ALIVE FOR A F

From Gaps to Significance

By Owusu Amoateng Kofi

Onwards and Upwards Publications
Berkeley House
11 Nightingale Crescent
West Horsley
Surrey
KT24 6PD
England

www.onwardsandupwards.org

ISBN: 978-1-907509-06-3

Cover design: Leah-Maarit

Printed in the UK

CONTENTS

DEDICATION

- To the young man or woman who thinks life is not worth living.

- To the person who is seeking to discover for himself.

- To the one seeking God's best idea for his or her life.

- To the one who have lost his purpose in life but is determined to rediscover what is lost or missing.

- To the purpose-seeking person who is willing to take what he or she has to the next dimension no matter how small it may look today.

ACKNOWLEDGMENTS

We are all who we are today because of what somebody thought of us yesterday. I am very grateful to men and women who have given me the permission to stand on their shoulders to be where I am today. Indeed the greatest way to motivate people is to step on the shoulders of previous generations.

I am also grateful for all my friends and colleagues in and outside the ministry, especially Nana Augustine for his unconditional support.

For the development and production of this book, I would like to especially thank:

- My special wife, **Rhoda and daughter Christine** for their prayer support and encouragement. Together we are fulfilling God's purpose for our lives.

- My father and mother, **Kofi Owusu and Stella,** whose lives have been an inspiration in my life for who and what I am today. Dad, I hope I have made you proud. I love you and will always remember you for what you have taught me. Also to my step mum, Monica, for all that you have done. Words are not enough to explain.

-

- To my two lovely sisters, **Benita and Marlis,** for your love and support. Marlis, your dedicated poem for the introduction of this book is perfect. Love you girls and everything you are doing.

- To **Ken Omeje, Andrea Onduku, Kwadwo Konadu** for their help in editing.

INTRODUCTION

At the age of 14, my younger sister (Marlis) wrote this poem: Alive for a Purpose.

ALIVE FOR A PURPOSE

"Alive for a purpose, alive for a purpose;
why did my mother give birth to me?
If I had died, I would be at rest by now
but am alive for a purpose.

Alive for a purpose, alive for a purpose;
why did my mother hold me at her knee?
Why did she feed me at her breast?
I would be sleeping by now, like the kings and rulers who built
ancient palaces, if I was not born
But I'm alive for a purpose.

Alive for a purpose;
why did I not die the moment that I was born?
By now I would be sleeping like a princess who filled her
houses with gold or silver or sleeping like a still born baby.
I wish I had died but then I could not carry out the purpose of
God after death.
So I am happy to be alive because I am
Alive for a purpose."

When she posted this poem to me, for the first time, every written word in this poem pierced my soul as I began to wonder how at such tender age this little girl could come out with such profound wisdom. Indeed, we are all alive because there is a purpose for our lives. *"Who am I? Why did I not die at birth? Why am I still alive after all that I have been through?"*are all questions that prove we are all alive for a reason?

This book is about the reasons you are alive. Alive for a Purpose simply means that life is worth living as long as there is breath in your nostrils and that you should be searching for the reason that will make you achieve greatness and fulfilment. For every achievement or accomplishment in life, there is a purpose and nothing else. No individual, group, organisation, nations, church, countries or tribe can succeed without purpose. Everything in the world is created for a reason. Nothing that He (GOD) made was for nothing. This explains why when a tree is cut down furniture can be made out the wood or when rocks are mined gold can be found or oil can be dredged from the sea. How much more man that God created in his image.

When you lose your purpose, life becomes uncontrollable and unbearable. You feel like a dead person even while though alive. **Myles Munroe (1992)** wrote in his book *The Pursuit of Purpose* that "**history shows that the value of life decreases and the quality of existence diminishes when a generation loses its sense of destiny and purpose.**"

This is true because everything in life that works is connected. Take a minute and look around you to see whether this is true. If your life is not working then you probably are disconnected. Purpose achieves because it gets you connected to who you are and explains to you the reason why you have been created.

We are all at different stages in life and whatever stage you find yourself, I believe you want the best out of life. The key to changing yourself effectively must first come from a change of your perception. If you are living a life of doubt and fear, then it is going to be difficult to live a purposeful life. God's code for effective living revolves around his basic principles for our lives. Developing personality and character ethics holds the key to effective illustration of Gods original intention for our lives. Things like integrity, humility, patience, simplicity shapes your character. Things like positive attitudes, determination, perseverance and courage shape your personality. As you begin to see things from the inside out rather than the outside in, what seems impossible comes alive.

Therefore, if you want to possess what God has freely given you, you must begin to change the central part of you into believing the **basic** principles God has set in the world. Based on these principles, this book throws more light on developing new levels of thinking that will help you to discover and rediscover purpose, fight through its challenges to attain new heights and dimension in your **work, personal and spiritual growth** and even in your **marriage**, because, just as **Albert Einstein** puts it, **"the significant problems we face cannot be solved at the same level of thinking we were at when we created them."**

In this book, three themes weave their way through as you read its pages. The first is about **discovering your purpose in life**. God's purpose for your life is already inside you from the day you were born. It is there waiting to be discovered so whether you are young or old, if you want to live a life of reason, you must first uncover what is covered in your life. The question too many of us ask is: *"What do I need to discover before I can achieve?"* This is what this book sets out to unleash. It is filled with people who have already discovered their purpose and living the on-purpose life.

The second is about **re-discovering your purpose in life**. The word re-discovery simply means that you had something **but you lost it**. There are people who have actually discovered their God given purpose in life but due to one reason or another, have missed their calling again. Whether it is because of life's obstacles, stress, depression or even the misunderstanding of the differences between your vision and ambition, this book seeks to bring you back online again. Earth has no sorrow God cannot solve. There are no problems or limitations God cannot fix for you. You can rediscover Gods original idea for your life.

The third theme will lead you to **get to your next level**. Many people ask the question: *"When I have discovered or re-discovered God's calling for my life, how then do I achieve?"* It is by always seeking to go to the next level. It is striving away from living in the familiar that will lead you into transformation. God has given you a talent or passion for something not just to bury it but to do something worthy with it. It takes divine wisdom, appreciating your talents, your passions and negotiating accordingly.

Life is a journey from 'gaps to significance' and it is what you do in the gap that determines how significant your life will become. It is only by working and making peace with your purpose that you fill this gap. This book combines **sound Christian biblical principles** with stories of men and women who dwelt on purpose to achieve significance in life; because what is life without a purpose.

As you read this book, my prayer for you, after every chapter, is this: **May you be restored in your soul, revived in your spirit, refreshed in your body and released into Gods divine calling for your life!**

CHAPTER 1
PURPOSE DEFINED

Two young men, **Kelvin** and **Melito,** are shoppers. As friends they enjoyed roaming from one shop to another, in their reserve times, buying and idolizing what was new on the market. One day, as they were in town doing what they did best, they entered into a big shopping mall. It so happened that both discovered a laptop on sale which both expressed an interest to buy. However, these were friends who had minimum paid jobs, whose salaries could not match the price of their laptop. The only way they could own the laptop was to save money overtime, something that would require perseverance, determination and focus on their side. It so happens that, after a period of eight months, Kelvin was able to save enough to purchase the laptop. On the other hand, Melito was unable to save enough to buy the laptop, even after several years had passed. His reason for not being able to acquire the laptop went beyond his inability to save alone.

> In between the moment, you identify something worthwhile to live and die for until the time you actually accomplish that reason is always a gap.

This short, but intriguing, story demonstrates to us **two** main categories of people, one of which you might fall into.

Firstly, we have the Kelvin group of people representing those who identify something in life and are able to derive the necessary drive that helps to accomplish their purpose in life. This group of people possess the strength, focus and determination to work on achieving success for what they discover in life. They also work hard towards a goal ahead of them.

Secondly, we have the Melito group of people who represent those who have a level of purpose but lack the necessary drive in order to succeed. This group are usually characterised by wishful thinking rather than a purpose driven life; for when purpose lacks the power to move you ahead to accomplish a goal, it can be defined as a wish. Wishes are feelings that sometimes exhibit the qualities of a purpose achieving life. They lack strength, perseverance and character to overturn what they see into what they want.

In between the moment you identify something worthwhile to live and die for until the time you actually accomplish it is always a gap. Filling that gap will lead your life to significance. Refusing to fill that gap will lead you to wonder what life is all about. What makes you fill this gap is what you are about to explore in this book. Though they had the same desires, Kelvin filled that gap but Melito could not. Kelvin's purchase of the laptop represents the significance of filling the gap, the joy of accomplishment, satisfaction and unimaginable feeling of actually finishing what he started.

❖ **What therefore is the purpose that drives me to actualize significance in my life and how do I achieve by such purpose?**

❖ **What are God's original idea (thinking) for my life and this planet?**

❖ **How do I move a wishful type of purpose to a more significant one?**

❖ **How do I discover or rediscover Gods reason for my life?**

❖ **How do I become effective in life?**

These are some of the questions I challenge you to begin to think and analyse in your heart and mind. Every individual has a natural desire to succeed in life. The reason simply being that you are Gods creation and whatever God creates simply wants to succeed but as to whether it will be a reality is as a result of your purpose in life. *"Who Am I? What Am I Doing with my Life? Why am I here?"* are questions you may have encountered in your life. Until now, these questions are the most difficult ones to answer. Refusing to answer these questions leads to abuse of purpose. Answering them too leads to fulfilment in life and achieving significance. *Which one do you want?* Make your own choice now before you continue reading. Richard Leider (1997, p2) conducted a research which suggested that after every decade an individual asks himself the three most important questions stated above. It usually come as a result of completion of a higher education and not knowing where to begin from in life or met by crisis in business or life or come to a point where the next seems gloomy or life becomes empty or futile.

WHAT THEREFORE IS PURPOSE?

Purpose is the strength to your vision. In other words, purpose is the footprint or steps to success. It is what switches you on and gives you the never-ending pursuit. It is what I call the meaning of life today to the life you desire tomorrow. It is what drives you anytime you wake up every morning from bed. It is what inspires you to do and give you the ideas that drive them. As wishes lead you to feel how good things may be like, purpose leads you to taste actual success.

As a child of God, purpose is also His perfect will for your life. It goes beyond permission to ultimate perfection, meaning it is Gods ultimate plan for your life. Purpose is also Gods created power within you that gives you understanding of what is important and worthwhile. It serves as a systematic guide to your destiny. It is important to understand that purpose cannot be chosen quickly. It has to be discovered! Discovering your purpose is an

> **As wishes lead you to feel how good things may be like, purpose leads you to taste actual success.**

inbuilt desire that when fulfilled brings joy and a drive to pursue it with excellence thus increasing one's overall happiness. It is in-built in your genetic make-up and leads you to discover the joy of the new and the pursuit of *excellence* in order to increase happiness in your life. A friend once told me, in a funny way, that purpose sometimes stops you from sleeping at night. It keeps you awake deep in the night and asks you questions: **"Who are you? What are you doing with your life?"**

Well I believe it is because when you are not living it out you do not really experience true joy and happiness. This is what this book leads you to realise and discover for yourself.

Most people find it difficult to understand the clarity of their purpose because of their lack of understanding the true meaning of **vision, ambition**, and **destiny**. When you know your vision, purpose follows and when you have known your purpose, you will understand when you have come to your destination. Understanding these forms a chief prerequisite for feeling the true joy of purpose. Let me shed some light on these three important principles.

Vision is usually defined as *what you see*! However, spiritually speaking, it is the miraculous revelation of God's truth. In other words, it is seeing beyond you. **"EQUIP", a Leadership Mandate Programme** by **John Maxwell**, defines vision as **"a clear mental picture of a better tomorrow, given by God, which moves a person to believe that it not only could be done, but it should be done."**

Nigel MacLennan (1999) explained: **"Vision has an end point of eight to twenty years in the future."** Vision is the Creator's original intention for your life. God created everything, including you, for a purpose. Nothing He made was without reason and because He created you, He has something for you that only He can show you. The first characteristic of a vision is that God gives it and in Gods vision lays His presence, power and purpose for your life. In it, you have a focus and a

> When you know your vision, purpose comes next and when you have known your purpose, you will understand when you have come to your destination.

clear picture of what you will look like and a sense of purpose. **"I know the plans I have for you. The plan of good and not of evil and one to bring you to an expected end, says the Lord."** (Jeremiah 29:11). When God said this, He meant what He sees in your life and can achieve in your life. So we can say that God's vision for your life becomes your purpose in life. Other characteristics of a divine vision are that its fulfilment rests on the individual's obedience. When it comes to such vision, others are seen as complementary and not competitors. When such vision is made known, discovering how to make it a reality can be elusive compared with other vision of our own making that seem easier to achieve. This is why the Bible says, **"The vision is for an appointed time, so though it may seem slow wait patiently, for it will surely not be delayed"** (Habakkuk 2:3). The path to achieving or fulfilling visions can often be long and we need to exercise patience. However, in the case of a divine vision, when it is finally fulfilled, it is satisfying, as it benefits people. It is people-centred, meaning that the focus of God's vision for a created life is to reach people and is not for the *carriers'* personal satisfaction. So Abraham, Jacob, Joseph, David etc all had it. So do you! As long as you remain a created vessel of the Creator, you have one!

<u>Ambition</u> can also simply be defined as *what you see*! What you see in your life, for instance in the eight to twenty years, can also be your ambition. To clarify more, ambition is what you personally choose to see in your life ahead of time. **Choice** and **interest** are key factors with this kind of vision. Bear in mind that ambition is still a vision but it is a **man-made vision**. Every child, when asked, will tell you what he sees himself doing when he grows up. He creates it based on his

gifts and **skills**. When God created you, He also gave you a choice. He has a reason for your life; yes, but choice also gives you the audacity to do something for yourself. So the ambition shapes as you grow. In **1 Thessalonians 4:11 NLT**, Paul makes a profound statement about ambition and I quote: "**This should be your ambition: to live a quiet life, minding your own business, and working with your hands, just as we commanded you before.**"

Therefore, everything about *ambition* is for your own personal satisfaction; to build yourself and generate revenue through your own business organisation, ideas and thinking. This explains why similar people or even organisations are viewed as competitors and are not complementary. When we look at the life of David, God's vision for his life made him a king but he personally was a shepherd boy **(1 Samuel 16:11).** Abraham's ambition made him a cattle-rearer but Gods vision took him to the Promised Land **(Genesis 13).** Paul was a tent maker but the vision for his life made him an apostle **(Acts 18:3).** Before Moses met God's vision for his life, he was successful in looking after sheep **(Exodus 3:1).** Jesus grew up learning to become a carpenter until the age of thirty when He started to fulfil His calling.

Destiny: Destiny comes from the word 'destination', which means the purpose for which something is destined. **Pastor Paul Scanlon (*Abundant Life Church, England*)** said this about destiny, "**It is the deeper part of you that always reminds you of who you are. Simply put, it is the real you**". He continued, **"You do not make your destiny, it makes you and you do not live it, it lives you. You do not put your destiny on,**

it puts you on. **Your destiny creates a kind of magnetisation over your life. It makes you sticky."**

This explains why there are times in your life when you feel something beyond you is pulling you to what you originally were meant to

Your calling, which is your purpose, is linked to your destiny.

be. Your destiny is your spirit man and that is why you cannot change it. When you step into your destiny, purpose follows and there is a feeling of faith and deep peace. In **Romans 8:29-30**, the Bible says something I believe explains the relationship between destiny and purpose.

"For whom He did foreknow, He also did predestine, conform to the image of His Son, that He might be the firstborn among many brethren. Moreover whom He did predestine, them He also called: and whom He called, them He also justified: and whom He justified, them He also glorified." Romans 8:29-30 (KJV).

What this verse is telling you is that God had your destiny planned even before He created you. That is what He means by **'He foreknew you'**. In **verse 30, 'whom He predestined'**, meaning in your spirit is your destiny and you are called. Your calling, which is your purpose, is also linked to your destiny. Therefore, when you live a purpose life, day in, day out, you fulfil your destiny at the end. To sum it up, I view destiny as the bigger picture and purpose as the day-to-day steps to fulfil destiny. When Jesus said, **"It is finished" (John 19:30)**, I believe He was talking about how, by living His calling or purpose for three years, He was led to fulfil His destiny. In the same way when Paul said, **"I have fought the good fight of** faith, I have finished the race." **(2 Timothy 4:7)** He was also referring to a fulfilled destiny because of living *on purpose* life.

Precious one, all these are important. That is why I have taken time to throw more light on the subject, so that you can now have a clearer picture of what this book is about. God has a vision for your life! You may be very ambitious and in your spirit lies the greatest you which is your destiny but to achieve and live from gaps to significance, you have to live by God's code, which is purpose.

Dr Myles Munroe (1992), pastor and author of "*The Pursuit of Purpose*" dived into the matter of purpose. He defined purpose as the "*master of all motivation and the mother of commitment. Purpose*", he said, "*is that which gives birth to hope and instils the passion to act. Purpose is the reason for being and the essence of existence. In other words it is the why that explain the reason for living.*"

> When you know what your purpose is and the values you need to develop to get to where you are going, your destiny becomes exciting.

The values we place on life and the decisions we make in life are what will separate us at the end and these two things shape our purpose in life. Still concentrating on the **Kelvin and Melito story**, both made the decision to buy the laptop but it was the value that Kelvin placed on it that made the difference. **Nigel MacLennan (1999, p69)** was right when he said, *"Purpose and value are strongly linked. Strong value and awesome purpose navigate you into the future, like an eternal burning beacon".* When you know what your purpose is and the values you need to develop to get to where you are going, your destiny becomes exciting. That is why **Carl and Stephanie** wrote, *"You must stop and reassess your priorities and values. You must be willing to be yourself, not what people want you to be because you think that is the only way you can get love. You are now at a point where, if you truly want to live, you have to be who you are."*

Purpose is all about revealing yourself. **Rene Daumal (1992)** captured the essence of purpose in his book *"Mount Analogue"* where he used mountains as metaphors for our own purpose stories. He wrote and I postulate, *"In the mythic tradition the mountain is the bond between Earth and Sky. Its solitary summit reaches the sphere of eternity, and its base spreads out in manifold foothills into the world of mortals. It is the way which man can raise himself to the divine and by which the divine can reveal itself to man."*

All of us need a purpose. Throughout the word of God, people's lives have depicted that God created man for a purpose.

Noah the shipbuilder was encouraged by purpose, because it was not raining when he started to build the ark. It was due to purpose that he was able to build the ark to save this sinful world

The modern corporate man still has purpose

Abraham's purpose was to establish and spread the belief that there was one God whose Spirit permeated through the entire universe because Abraham was living in a time where people were divided to serving different gods. So through Abraham God established His purpose for the world.

Moses' purpose was to lead the Hebrews out of captivity from Egypt to the Promised Land. Joshua actually led them into the Promised Land. David's purpose was to win battles to demonstrate God's sovereignty and power to his enemies. Solomon built God's temple to demonstrate God's glory and purpose. The aim of all the Prophets was to help keep and restore the nations to Gods original purpose.

The modern corporate man still has purpose and in the next chapter, we focus our attention on ordinary people who have discovered theirs and fulfilled them.

KEY LESSONS AND PRINCIPLES

➢ Life is a journey made up of gaps and significance. Filling the gaps will lead you to significance, ignoring to fill this gap will make you a walking generality.

➢ As wishes lead you to feel how good life can become, purpose leads you to taste actual success.

PURPOSE DEFINED

1. Purpose is the strength to your vision.
2. Purpose is God's perfect will for your life.
3. Purpose is God's created power within you that gives you an understanding of what is important and worthwhile.
4. Purpose is a systematic guide to your destiny.
5. Purpose is your day-to-day steps to fulfil your destiny.
6. Purpose is what switches you on and give you the drive to achieve.
7. Purpose is the meaning of life today to give you a better tomorrow.
8. Purpose is the discovery of the new and pursuing it in excellence to accomplish happiness in once lifetime.
9. Purpose explains who you are, why you are born and what you have been born for.
10. Purpose is the master of all motivation, the mother of all commitment.

➢ Everything in life has a purpose, including you.

➢ The values we place in life and the decisions we make is what separates us and shape our purpose.

CHAPTER 2
PURPOSE PICTURED

There are a very few chapters in this book where you will find a sort of prelude to them. This is one of them and it is because of its importance. As you read this book, you will discover real life stories as a tool for influence about purpose. The fundamental aim in this chapter is to create a perfect picture in your mind as to what purpose is or is not about and to challenge you in your calling because the human mind thinks in pictures. We are visual people living in a visual age. Just as Jean Anouilh said, "**Fiction gives life its form.**"

The best of human experience can serve as the most powerful form of human communication. No wonder the Bible is the most sought after book in the world. People read it because it contains stories of real life situations of people we can most of the times identify ourselves with. "**God made man because he loved stories" (Isak Dinesen)**. I believe this statement is true because through your story God can communicate and challenge others. Have you ever asked yourself why Jesus used so many stories, riddles and parables to communicate to others? He used them to get their attention and to create a perfect image of what He needed to get across. In **Revelation 12:11,** the Bible says, "**They overcame him by the blood and by the word of their testimony.**" Notice that it is not only through the blood of Jesus that you can overcome;

> **Through your story, God can communicate and challenge others.**

you can also overcome by the sharing of your testimony, which can be your story so far. Let us turn our imagination and picture perfectly, not only biblical characters but also men and women, in the secular world today whose lives depict those in the Bible. I pray that this will guide you on your journey from gaps to significance and if God loves stories, as Isak Dinesen said, what is your story because someone is waiting to hear yours to begin his.

My Uncle's Story

I had an uncle who was paralysed for almost six years after which he died. Before he died, I saw the agony and meaningless life he had because of his sickness. As I write on the issue of purpose, my retentiveness is just taking me back to his days and God, I believe, is using my uncle's life to inspire this book. Yes, until his death, my uncle could see, breathe, eats, talk a little but could not move to do the things he wanted to do.

Life without purpose is like your body without a functioning spinal cord.

As time went on, he became frustrated because life became purposeless and meaningless. All he could do was to sit in his wheelchair everyday for six years and wait for somebody to push him around. He suffered from a nervous breakdown of the spinal cord, the human body supporting system. Simply put: **it is the backbone to your body system**. It functions by sending information from the brain down to the nerves. Now imagine your spinal cord is damaged. A complete injury means that there is no function below the level of the injury; no sensation and no voluntary movement. Both sides of the body are equally affected. When this transpires, it is usually said one has become paralysed for life. **You then wonder why and what you are living for?** This is simply what happened to my uncle but as I write I want you to compare this to a life without purpose.

In life, your purpose functions just like the spinal cord. As long as you are able to envision what and why you were created there will always be meaning and movement in life. If not, you will just go about everyday like someone with an injured spinal cord, always busy but without meaning or fulfilment in life. That is why most of us find ourselves busy but inside we keep ask ourselves why. **Henry David Thoreau** honestly put it; **"It is not enough to be busy. Ants are busy. The question we should ask ourselves is what are we busy about?"** Life without purpose is like a body without a functioning spinal cord. In life, you need a backbone and not a wishbone. For every accomplishment, there is a purpose and not a wish.

In my uncle's life I saw that we were born as purpose seeking individuals. Purpose is a necessity for our health and survival. His illness contributed to his death mainly because he ceased to have purpose and meaning. Research suggests that rates of illness and death increase when man gives up their sense of purpose.

Jessica Cox Story

I read an article from the Monday, December 8, 2008 **UK Metro newspaper**, which read *"Pilot who Flies by her*

Feet." It was about a young woman whose story depicts that of real purpose and this was what was said,

*"'**Determined Jessica Cox'**, she is called. A twenty five year old was born with a generic defect, meaning she was born without arms. Ms Cox from Tucson, Arizona (USA) a graduate and holder of a double black belt in Tae Kwon-do. 'I have taught myself how to write, type, drive a car, brush my hair and use the phone simply by using my feet.' Recently, she has gone forward to overcome her fear of flying and a profound disability becoming the first person ever to pilot a plane using only her feet. She said I am in complete control and that is invigorating. I literally have my life in my hand or should I say my feet. Though it took her 3 years, instead of the usual 6 months, to complete her lightweight aircraft licence, today she has done it. Today, her purpose in life is to instruct other disabled people how to fly.* **"I never say I can't do that, I just say I have not worked it out yet,"** *she said.*

This woman's life is a challenge to everyone. Though having a profound disability, she had not given up on purpose compared to many others who have. She had all the excuses to lay back and do nothing other than claim benefits from the government or beg for bread. Instead she demonstrated to us that no matter what your situation is, God has a purpose for you. Jessica reminds me of what Jesus said, in John 9:3, to His disciples. One day when the Master was walking along with His disciples, they met a disabled man with blindness from birth. His disciples then asked why some people are born with disabilities, just like Jessica. Jesus replied and said, **"It is not because of their sin or their parent's sin but for the power of God to be seen in them."** Therefore, it is no wonder that in

Jessica we see the power of purpose. Let her life challenge yours.

Joni Eareckson Story

If you think Jessica's story is not inspirational enough, then pay attention to the life of Joni Eareckson Tada. A diving accident in 1967 left Joni Eareckson , a quadriplegic, in a wheelchair. As a teenager, Joni loved life. She enjoyed riding horses and loved to swim. One summer, in 1967, all that changed. While swimming with some friends, Joni, dove into a lake not knowing how shallow it really was. She broke her neck, paralyzing her body from the neck down. For the next two years, during her rehabilitation, Joni struggled. She struggled with life, she struggled with God and she struggled with her paralysis. Since then, Joni has written fourteen books, has recorded several musical albums and is actively involved as an advocate for disabled people.

You may be wondering how she has done this. I read her story, from her website and her book **"Joni"**, which has been distributed in many languages and which has been made into a feature film. According to her story, she believes that when this unfortunate accident happened, the devil's agenda was to shipwreck her faith, dash her hopes, ruin her family, destroy her dreams and destroy her belief in God. Nevertheless, after the period of shock and grief over what she had lost, she remembered that we have an all-wise, all-powerful, all loving God who reaches down to glorify himself in such situations. She knew that through this accident, God had a purpose, a plan that He would manifest despite the accident that left her paralysed. According to Joni, God used the accident to turn a headstrong, stubborn, rebellious kid into a young woman who would reflect patience, endurance and long-suffering.

This is not to say that Joni saw any glory in suffering a spinal cord injury, cerebral palsy, muscular dystrophy, multiple sclerosis, cystic fibrosis, brain injury, stroke, heart disease or manic depression. There is no gladness or joy in these things. Though a mystery, Joni believed that it was not a mystery without direction. As said in **Romans 8:28,** all things can fit together into a pattern, a plan for good, for our good and His glory. Joni glorified God in the midst of all that she went through.

She says that while still in hospital continuing in her recovery, other things began to matter to her than the things that had previously seemed so important when she was on her feet such as patience, endurance, self-control, steadfastness, love and joy. She began to see herself differently, somebody special, somebody significant and she began to share the word of God. She began to take courage in the word of God. 1 Corinthians 15 also came alive to her which states that one day we will all have new hands, new legs that will walk, new hearts and new minds. Though she has faced a lot of limitation living in a wheel chair for over twenty six years, she has found limitless joy and peace in knowing Jesus Christ. For more of Joni's story, visit **www.Joniearecksontadastory.com** (accessed December, 2009).

Today, Joni Tada is the founder of Joni and Friends (JAF) in 1979, an organisation for Christian ministry in the disability community throughout the world. The organisation grew into the establishment in 2006 of **Joni and Friends International**

Disability Centre (IDC). Joni is married to her husband Ken since 1982. Joni Tada's purpose today is to use her story and experience to demonstrate to us how a personal relationship with God has helped her overcome the obstacles in her life and how you can experience the love of God, despite pain and suffering.

My father's story

When I was growing up, one person I grasped so much from was my father. We would sit down and talk about things that, as a child, I saw but never really understood and he would take his time to explain them to me. I personally also observed his life from a distance throughout my growing up with him so there were things I gained from him without him even knowing. One of the things about picturing the lives of people you respect is that you grow wise from doing so and it helps you to shape your own purpose in life.

I was nine years of age when I lost my mother. At that unfortunate moment, I recall my two sisters were barely three years and one year old respectively. When this happened, I stood there and watched the tears in my father's eyes. In his eyes, I could perceive frustration together with pain and lack of drive to live on. As young as I was, I could understand why but I still thought there was something more than just weeping for a lost wife. My mum was virtually the bread winner of the family in those days because she had the best job with the best pay while my dad would have described himself as a young man, in his early thirties, without much of a purpose.

Therefore, when Mum passed away, it was a wake-up call for him to begin to do something worthwhile in his life especially when the extended family also gave up on us. So what had been a painful death of a lovely, supportive wife became a challenge factor for my dad.

> You will not always find your calling wrapped up in a loving caring situation. Sometimes the situation may not be that which is palatable to you

As the years went by and as a teenager, I discovered a dramatic change in my dad. Determination and focus to raise his children to become great personalities in the future became the purpose of my father. He wanted the three of us to go for gold so he purposed in his life to give us a university education, no matter what the cost. So in my formidable years, I recall dad entering into business. He first started as middle salesperson, introducing and mediating between clients and sellers and gaining commissions when there happened to be a business transaction between them. After a considerably period, he saved enough to purchase a van to transport the goods clients had purchased after he had mediated for them. This helped him to take care of his family and to save. After years of working as intermediary and a driver, the Lord granted him favour to open his own business as a retailer with what he had saved. He had also become trustworthy among most wholesalers he had worked for so he had the opportunity of buying on credit and paying later.

By the time I entered into university, Dad had gone ahead to establish a second shop to expand his business and by the time I completed my degree, he had completed his housing project for the family and was ready to push my sisters onto university.

Unfortunately, my dad passed away at a painful age of fifty but today we look back at his life with gratitude and with honour, more than we do with sorrow. You may ask why? Because when we look back into his years, we see a man who achieved his purpose in life. Not only did we benefit from such purpose, others too did.

My father's story, I believe, does not only challenge his children but to you as well. I now understand that God can even use life's crisis to bring out your purpose in life. There is nothing impossible to God. You will not always find your calling wrapped up in a loving caring situation. Sometimes the situation may not be that which is palatable to you, it may be through bitter encounter but if you should hold on, God can transform your life. His story also has convinced me that you do not need so many years to finish the task ahead of you because if I look at what my dad accomplished in matter of fifty years, it is unbelievable. Similarly today, you find many older people who live with no purpose. It took Jesus thirty three years to accomplish His purpose on earth. If a man spends his precious time and energy wisely through purpose, he will live an organised life.

In these four stories lay a perfect picture of what purpose is and what it is not.

❖   **From my uncle's situation we learn that** :

You can be busy but to no end. Purpose is not simply doing just anything but what you are *created* to do. My uncle gave up quickly compared to the others, in this chapter, and this contributed to his demise. If he had remained positive and responded to the truth that all things work together for good, perhaps God could have worked through him to affect his generation in a much deeper sense. Many more people are in my uncle's state today may be thinking of giving up.

❖ **To all such people I pray that:**

You can learn from Joni Eareckson Tada and still discover Gods purpose for your life because in the midst of pain, stress or anxiety, God is able to do exceedingly and abundantly above what you think.

❖ **Most importantly**: There are able-bodied men and women in our time today who, though physically fit, are acting like broken spinal cords with no purpose. To such people, activate true purpose and focus on the main things.

To sum up this chapter: Whether you have been born with any genetic disability, learn from Jessica Fox who demonstrates determination and optimism. Whether you have become disabled through injury or anything, learn from Joni who said, **"Let other things begin to matter to you; patience, endurance, tolerance, self-control, steadfastness, sensitivity, love and joy."** For this is what purpose is all about. To the man or woman, in one crisis or other, my dad's story can be an example. For if you look well, in that crisis, you can discover Gods best ideals for your life.

KEY LESSONS AND PRINCIPLES

➢　　God wants to use your purpose to communicate and challenge others to stop giving up and start stepping up.

➢　　Understanding purpose is a mystery but not a mystery without direction.

➢　　Life without purpose is like a broken spinal cord.

➢　　In shaping your purpose, picture successful people and learn from them.

➢　　Crisis is a mirror of purpose.

CHAPTER 3
PURPOSE AND TIME (Duration)

"We are all born originals. Why is it that most of us die copies" (John Mason).

Everything in life has a purpose. From the beginning of the world, the Bible assures us that God created everything for a purpose in its original form **(Genesis 1:26-28 KJV):**

'And God said, "Let us make man in our image, after our likeness; and let them have dominion over the fish of the sea, and over the fowl of the air, and over the cattle, and over all the earth, and over every creeping thing that creepeth upon the earth." So God created man in His *own* image, in the image of God created He them; male and female created He them. And God blessed them, and God said unto them, "Be fruitful, and multiply, and replenish the earth, and subdue it: and have dominion over the fish of the sea, and over the fowl of the air, and over every living thing that moveth upon the earth."

We understand that God created man with special intentions. God's original intention for man was to cause man to have godly qualities over everything He created. This means that you are born in the image of God. Having godly qualities is also doing the things that God can do and to reflect His originality. In **verse 28**, we discover that God also created

Man is officially mandated to be fruitful, multiply, replenish and subdue the earth.

man to have dominion over creation and this is where your purpose lies. The word **'dominion'** is to have **'an official order to rule or reign over something'**. Therefore, we have been officially created to do something and identifying that very thing becomes your purpose. So, in **verse 28**, whoever you are and wherever you find yourself, it is the understanding of this that *purpose* creates in you. Whatever you do, you should be aiming towards these four things mentioned above because they form the basis to your purpose.

Everything in life has a purpose.

Until you get Gods original plan for your life, anything you do is an assumption. So **nothing** that God made was a copy or without reason. Purpose is in everything. It is just waiting to be unveiled, to be fruitful and to multiply. The word **'creates'** means **'to make something out of nothing'**, meaning you are unique and special. Everything visible that God created came from things eyes cannot see. The presence of the Lord commanded things to come forth and it happened because of who He is and what He does. Therefore, you are not from trees or even monkeys as scientist try to convince you. You have been created from the invisible things of this world and not made from trees or monkeys. This explains the originality of everything the hand of God has made including man who is both male and female.

The next question I want you to think about is this: **"If God created you and you are original, then is there something that you are here to do and only you can do?"**

Your originality from creation by God means that there is something you have to donate and there is a timeframe for you to give this particular thing out. What do I mean by this?

The Bible says that one day **Jesus** and His disciples were passing by and on the way they saw a blind man whom He later healed. The disciples asked Him a question **(John 9:2-4 NLT):**

> **"Teacher,"** His disciples asked Him, **"Why was this man born blind? Was it a result of his own sins or those of his parents?" "It was not because of his sins or his parents' sins,"** Jesus answered. **"He was born blind so the power of God could be seen in him. All of us must quickly carry out the tasks assigned us by the One who sent me because there is little time left before the night falls and all work comes to an end."**

By Jesus saying this, He was referring to the purpose why God created us all. In Jesus' statement lies the key to achieving significance in life. There are four things in this statement you can adapt.

1.   God has created all of us for a reason:

We have all been created to do something unique and peculiar to our calling in life. That is why Jesus said someone (God) has sent us and we must do the reason He has sent us. You have been created for a reason and that reason should be fulfilled. Remember you did not just happen, God especially made you happen. You must be fruitful, multiply, replenish and subdue in your generation.

2. There is duration to that thing God wants you to do.

Creation has a beginning and an end. There is a timeframe for you to achieve God's purpose for your life and since you will not live forever, you must begin to think about what God has created you to do. The Bible says in **Hebrews 9:23** that, **"it is appointed for man to live once after that judgment."** There is a time to be born and a time to die.

3. We must act quickly.

Because our duration is limited by the day, we must act quickly. By Jesus referring to *the day*, he meant that there is no time to waste on unnecessary things. You must find your calling as soon as you can and begin to donate in relation to your purpose.

4. We are stewards.

You are the caretaker of your life, and to what God has freely given you. Jesus is still calling to you to live right and dwell on the power of purpose to discover your essence in life. For as stewards you are called to give account of how you used your God given gifts and talents whether you added value to them or not or whether you buried them. This is why He said night will come when no one will be able to do anything. **'Night'** here represents **"a time when all-purpose will cease"**. Eternity has no beginning or end and it's outside of any duration or time. Your duration on earth starts from when you are born to when you will die which you don't know when.

The word **'duration'** according to the dictionary means **'the length of time something continues or exists or the continuance in time'**. In philosophy, it is **'a temporal continuum, intuitively known within which élan vital operates'**. The word **'élan'** means **'to operate in vigour or enthusiasm or with seriousness'**. If we consider especially the philosophical definition of the word **'duration'**, we find out that man has a timeframe in which he lives and this is temporal. Within this time bound, we have to operate in vigour, enthusiasm, and with a reason. Without this reason then our entire life will be meaningless. This is what **John 9:4** purely means.

The problem I observe today is that most people operate under the **grasshopper mentality**, which is the feeling mostly young people have while growing up. Young adults often feel that there is more time ahead so will neglect opportunities to fulfil their purpose in life on time. On the other hand, the **grasshopper mentality** can

> The grasshopper mentality says that there is more time to achieve our purpose in life.

also affect other age groups as well. For instance, take a growing adult maturing in a fearing, intimidating and frustrating environment. Even after maturity, such fears still hold and keep the person from fulfilling their calling.

When you allow negative statements, unrealistic fears and insecurities to override your mental consciousness, you can be affected with this mentality of *more time.*

*A story has it that in a village, a violent strong wind blew and after things had calmed down, a boy went under a mango tree to pick mangoes. When he went, he was stunned to find out that there were fresh or unripe green mangos together with fully-grown ripe ones. In his mind, he thought that only ripe mangos should fall because they were the mature ones. He could not fathom this so he rushed back home and asked his grandfather why. The grandfather simply replied to him, "**In life the green falls and the old falls,**" meaning that in life a young man (green) dies and the old man dies (author unknown).*

This is a simple wisdom of what life is all about. You think you are young. Yes, it may be true but the most important question in life is: **"What are you using your life to do right now?"**

"No one knows when your night will come," said Jesus. God formed you for a reason and purpose. Things do not just happen. Things are made to happen.

> Use your God given purpose while it is day rather than night

There is a man named in the Bible whose life, I believe, is a lesson to us all. His name is **Methuselah**. This man's name appears only once in the Bible. All that is said about him in **Genesis 9:26-27** is that Methuselah lived for 969 years and he died. When this man's name is mentioned, all that we know is that he lived long and he died. The big question is: **"DO YOU WANT THIS to be SAID OF YOU?"**

Jesus Christ, the son of the living God lived for thirty three years. His life is an example for all of us to follow. For the Bible says that the **"Son of Man came to serve, not to be served and to give His life as a ransom to others."** Every step He took was a step of purpose. At the age of thirty, He entered into full ministry. At thirty three years of age, He said," **It is finished**," and He left. May be He was the Son of the living God or God Himself who came down knowing exactly what to do. Yes, He was special but, believe me, we are also special too. As it is written, **"We are all born for a reason."**

Luke 6:40 says,

"A student is not above his teacher but when he is fully trained he becomes like his teacher."

Yes, we are not Him but we can be like Him. If His life had meaning we can also have meaning. If He achieved we can also achieve. If He died saying, "It is finished," we can also die saying the same words. On the other hand just as He endured for a specific period we also must remember there is a time bomb we are also sitting on. It all begins by getting that full training. **'Training'** here means **'finding who you are and why you have been created'.** By Jesus saying this I believe He meant that though He is above you, if you trust and fully search in Him, you can also serve with purpose like Him and even achieve more.

As we speak of time **(duration)** and its essence on purpose, I would like us to understand the types of time. The ancient Greek has two words for time:

Chronos and Kairos

CHRONOS: refers to the chronological or sequential order of time or a moment of determined period. It is a time that can be measured; for instance, the time you start work and close from work. If you start work at 6am and close your work at 6pm, such working hours can be measured as a twelve hour shift simply by calculating the number of hours worked. If you complete a distance of 1 mile in ten minutes, such a time is deemed a measureable time. *Chronos* can therefore be defined as the qualitative nature of time. We all face *chronos* moments in our lives each day. Jesus is advising His disciples, in **John 9:4.** He was also warning them of their daily activities. Like in the words of **Frederic Hudson** and **Pamela Mclean,** "**Purpose is a profound commitment to the compelling expectation for the time of your life**"

> "He who has time to burn will never give the world much light. Killing time is not murder, it is suicide"
> Myles Munroe

Many of us do not even notice the time that we can measure. All we do is to complain, saying we don't have time enough to take care of our lives and purposes. For remember, as **Myles Munroe (1992, p 66)** said, **"He who has time to burn will never give the world much light. Killing time is not murder, it is suicide."** If you are missing out on the times you see passing by, what about the ones you cannot control. Since *chronos* can be measured, it is important to reassess yourself. Jesus in his advice is calling on us to measure some of our activities to see if we can let go of some work to focus on a much deeper calling. As

Matthew Fox puts it and I postulate, "**In our time we workers are being called to re-examine our work: how we do it, whom it is helping or hurting, what it is we do and what we might do if we were to let go of our present work and follow a deeper call.**" I hope it will be your priority now to say this prayer right now before you continue reading. "**Lord, teach me to number my days aright that I may gain a heart of wisdom**" (Psalm 90:12).

KAIROS: Karois is "**the moment of undetermined period in which something special happens.**" It is the ability to take advantage of changing, contingent

> One thing that precedes time is seasons

circumstances, a passing instant when an opening appears which must be driven through with force if success is to be achieved. Jesus in John 9:4 was teaching and at the same time warning his disciples about how to seize this moment, the moment to use their God given purposes whilst it is day rather than night. The day is when you have the opportunity to seize the moments in your lives and the night is when it has become too late to seize those moments.

I bet you that people who take the initiative and work hard fulfil their calling in life whilst it is still day but those who do not work hard towards seizing the moments of their lives are almost guaranteed to fail while it becomes night. Whoever you are just like in the words of **John Maxwell (2007, p 53)** there is, "**a decision you should be making, a problem you should be solving, a possibility you should be examining, a project you should be starting, a** goal you should be reaching, an opportunity you should be seizing and a dream you should be fulfilling."

These decisions, possibilities, projects, goals are the moments of your life you should be aiming to reach before you miss them. Unfortunately, many of us want to wait until everything is perfect or when everything becomes visible before we act. If you are part of such people then this book comes to warn you to open your eyes to the undetermined periods in your lives that God has availed to you. For as **John Maxwell (2007, p 53)** again asserted, **"It is better to be eighty percent sure and make things happen than it is to wait until you are one hundred percent sure because by then, the opportunities will have already passed you by."**

It is important to note that *kairos* times appears when we least expect. That is why you do not have to be a hundred percent positive before you begin to take them. It cannot be measured so you always have to be on the look-out. In **Ecclesiastes 3**, Solomon, the wisest man ever to have lived, spoke about time. Since it is said, **"a wise man learns from his own mistakes, the wiser man learns from other people's mistake but the wisest man learns from other people's success,"** I want you to learn from the wisest man and his lessons of time.

Ecclesiastes 3:1-11 (NLT):

"There is a time for everything, a season for every activity under heaven, a time to be born and a time to die, a time to plant and a time to harvest, a time to kill and a time to heal, a time to tear down and a time to rebuild, a time to cry and a time to laugh, a time to grieve and a time to dance, a time to scatter stones and a time to gather stones, a time to embrace and a time to turn away,

a time to search and a time to lose, a time to keep and a time throw away, a time to tear and a time to mend, a time to be quiet and a time to speak up, a time to love and a time to hate, a time for war and a time for peace. What do people really get for all their hard work? I have thought about this in connection with the various kinds of work God has given people to do. God has made everything beautiful for its own time. He has planted eternity in the human heart, but even so, people cannot see the whole scope of God's work from beginning to end."

It is important to note from Solomon's point of view that God has a purpose for everything under the sun. God's purpose is release in seasons and that is one reason why you do not have to wait until things are perfect before you decide to move. In **verse 1** it says, **"There is a season for every activity on earth."** This means the one thing that precedes time is seasons. For instance, in a season of rain is a time to grow and reap a bounty harvest, the winter season is a time of wearing heavy cloths. In the same way, there may be seasons in your life when you should be taking some important

> **Life is not measured by duration (time) but by donation (what you give).**

decisions in your life, fulfilling a dream or a calling, or beginning a project. It is a time for you to drive through the force and achieve success. The sad thing is that when we miss our seasons we miss our purpose. When a farmer misses the rainy season he reduces his productivity. In the same way, when you miss the summer, you miss the period of wearing summer cloths. So it is when we miss our *kairos* moment, we miss a time of fulfilling a purpose.

DONATION: The word simply means '**to give**'. It is also '**to present, bestow, contribute to something**' and that thing is life. We need to understand that we have been created to give and contribute our life to the world. This is what makes our life worthy. This is life's value. Ask yourself,

❖ what is life without contribution?

❖ What is life without giving?

> Your purpose in life is covered simply for you to discover. It is your choice to either search to occupy space or stop to occupy nothing.

God in his original intent has bestowed a responsibility on you to do something with your life today. This is the purpose I am drawing your mind to and you are alive for this very reason.

I know most people do not know what to donate. I meet people daily who simply think that though they have tried, they still cannot find their true purpose in life. For some they see themselves as having little to offer the world. The biggest question about purpose most people pose is this: **"If God really created us for a purpose and He expects us to contribute, how come this purpose is not easy to find out?"**

We are born and for the majority of us we do anything that comes our way. As humans we do not seem to easily know Gods will for our lives. For those who simply do not know the will of God for their lives and those who think that it is never easy to find your calling in life, I would like to say that **life is a spiral; growth does not come on a straight path**. The word *'spiral'* means 'a plane curve generated by a point moving around a fixed point while constantly receding from or approaching it'.** The spiral aspect related to life here is that life does not draw a straight line. Like the shell of a snail, thus life is like. A snail's shell constantly is spherical in nature and this can be compared to life's

Understanding purpose is to have the power to comprehend, or to achieve a grasp

purpose. Purpose is in you. It needs to be discovered. It is a life-long matter so it is not something you can simply say you have arrived at. If you are looking forward to find the results of life on a silver platter, then you will never find it easily like that. In the Bible when God gave free manna and meat to the Israelites, a time came that they did not appreciate what God did for them. Read the entire account in **Numbers 11.** If they had worked for that manna, would they have complained so bitterly? This is the nature of humans in general.

Should God release our purpose to us on a silver platter, most of us would behave like the Israelites. Look at how, even in our homes, we treat the things we buy cheaply or easily and the things we buy expensively or with difficulty. We treat expensive things with care more than cheaper ones. This is how, I believe, God has made your purpose. He has hidden it for you and not from you in a way. For since the time God stopped given manna He has said in **Proverbs 25:2** that "**it is the glory of God to conceal a matter and the glory of man to search for this matter.**"

It is simply Gods glory to conceal. And what does God conceal? A matter, and what is a matter? "**Matter is anything that has weight and can occupy space**." So before God, anything that has weight and can occupy space in life is concealed. '**To conceal**' simply means '**to hide**'. The big question coming here again is this: Why does God conceal? The answer is found in the same Proverbs 25:2. It is because of His *GLORY*. The glory of God is what makes God who He is and what He is.

What you are called to do is your purpose in life and the very thing you need to donate is a matter to God. It carries weight and can occupy space. Beloved, your life is a big matter to God and He deems it His glory, not just to hand it over to you cheaply but for you to search for it. For physical examples, you can think of all the important things in life and how they are found. Look at gold, bauxite, diamond, petrol and more. These things are not raised on the surface of the earth but by those who persevere and determine to search beyond the earth's surface.

The second part of the verse calls on man to gain glory by searching for what is a matter in his life. If by God concealing your purpose makes Him glorious, then you searching make you glorious too. Life is a quest and the man who solves life's quest finds answers. Your purpose in life is covered simply for you to discover. It is your choice to either search to occupy space or never search to occupy nothing.

He further explains to us how our purpose is in the **twenty-fifth chapter** of the same **Proverbs**: "**The purpose of man is like dark waters, a man of understanding brings it out" (Proverbs 20:5).**

Here God is likening your purpose in life to that of *dark waters*. Dark waters are synonymous to *dark matters*. Which is a matter that has not yet been detected or hidden from the masses? The **second section** of the verse says, *"A man of understanding will draw them near,"* meaning that you who understand can only bring what has been hypothesized to existence. It has not been detected and is hidden from light by the original Creator. To those who think life's purpose is not easy to find, this is my explanation to them. The road is always not easy but the one who searches finds, the one who knocks has open doors, the one who asks will be answered. Awareness of the pattern is all you need to sustain you along the way.

KEY LESSONS AND PRINCIPLES

➤ Everything in life has a purpose because God created man to have dominion.

➤ One must seize moments of opportunity to fulfil purpose.

➤ Seasons precede time and missing your season is missing your purpose.

➤ Life is a spiral; growth does not come on a straight path. Purpose is discovered overtime so that it will be cherished and fulfilled.

➤ Man is officially mandated to be fruitful, multiply, replenish and subdue the earth. This is Gods special intention for you.

➤ All men span (timeframe) for a specific moment and are expected to donate (give) in their lifetime of influence.

➤ Purpose is using your talents and a gift to influence while it is day, for night is coming where everything will stop.

➤ What defines God is His glory to hide things that matter. What defines you glorious is your ability to find out the matter God has originally hidden not from you but for you.

➤ Your purpose in life is covered simply for you to discover. It is your choice to either search to occupy space or stop to occupy nothing.

CHAPTER 4
THE ON-PURPOSE MAN

"What lies behind us and what lies before us are tiny matters, compared to what lies within us" (**Oliver Wendel Homes**).

Life begins with questions, questions about how to pursue that which lies within us. Nothing shapes our lives as much as that we want to straight from our hearts. That which lies deep within us is only executed by purpose since it is

> God's power is the power of purpose.

that which keeps us from giving up. We still develop fresh resolutions each year with the belief of bringing out that which God has put within us. God's power is the power of purpose.

As Paul stated in **Ephesians 3:20**: **"that glory be to God by His power that lies within us. He is able to accomplish more than we will ever dare to ask or hope"**.

This power within us challenges us to move forward each time until we have achieved our desires. This power, in **Ephesians 3:20,** represents our purpose in life. Behind every great accomplishment is this purpose of creativity that season our lives and makes it tasty and pleasant to live. We, therefore, view a man with purpose as being challenged to do things even more than the ordinary person will do.

Come with me in your imagination into the Bible to learn from a man whose purpose challenged him to go that extra mile beyond the ordinary. He is the servant of Abraham. The Bible says that Abraham was about to die and he needed a wife for his son Isaac. Therefore, he sent his faithful servant on a mission to search out a wife for his son. This mission became his purpose. That, which was within him, stretched him to go beyond the ordinary. As we use this biblical illustration, I will use an acrostic to explain to you what the sense of purpose in a man's life can make him do.

Genesis 24:9-22 (NLT):

"So, the servant took a solemn oath that he would follow Abraham's instructions. He loaded ten of Abraham's camels with gifts and set out, taking with him the best of everything his master owned. He travelled to Aram-naharaim and went to the village where Abraham's brother Nahor had settled. There the servant made the camels kneel down beside a well just outside the village. It was evening, and the women were coming out to draw water.

"O Lord, God of my master," he prayed, "give me success and show kindness to my master, Abraham. Help me to accomplish the purpose of my journey. See, here I am, standing beside this spring and the young women of the village are coming out to draw water. This is my request. I will ask one of them for a drink. If she says, 'Yes, certainly and I will water your camels, too!'—let her be the

one you have appointed as Isaac's wife. By this I will know that you have shown kindness to my master."

As he was still praying, a young woman named Rebekah arrived with a water jug on her shoulder. Her father was Bethuel, who was the son of Abraham's brother Nahor and his wife, Milcah. Now Rebekah was very beautiful and she was a virgin; no man had ever slept with her. She went down to the spring, filled her jug, and came up again. Running over to her, the servant asked, "Please give me a drink."

"Certainly, sir," she said, and she quickly lowered the jug for him to drink. When he had finished, she said, "I'll draw water for your camels, too, until they have had enough!" So she quickly emptied the jug into the watering trough and ran down to the well again. She kept carrying water to the camels until they had finished drinking. The servant watched her in silence, wondering whether or not she was the one the Lord intended him to meet. Then at last, when the camels had finished drinking, he gave her a gold ring for her nose and two large gold bracelets for her wrists."

Your journey to your destination in life can only be pursued with prayer.

In this story, we can identify seven major things in the life of a man living on purpose or on his way to discover significance.

❖ **The first thing** we learn from this servant is **PRAYER.** A man of purpose prays. Prayer is the number one key to unlock your God given purpose in life. Because He created you and knows your end from your beginning, He is the best to talk to and the only way to talk to Him is to pray. Prayer is man-having dominion on earth but calls on God to have influence in his dominion. God created man for earth, to have the same impact He has in heaven. God expects man to use his authority on earth because we are created in His image but there comes a time when man may be confronted with a situation beyond his control. During this period, man can call on God to grant him the permission to interfere in earthly matters, and this is when prayer becomes a key. With prayer, God will never break his laid down principle. I have always likened God to an *electric pole*. An electricity pole might be close to your house but if you do not take care, you may not have electricity in your house. This pole will neither force itself to your house nor ask you to draw power from it. Until you have bought the right connections and asked an electrical engineer to draw that power in to your home, you will continue to be powerless with the electrical energy. It is so with God; until you have called on Him to come into your dominion, you will still wonder from one place to the other though He is closer to you. One thing God gave you and me is **choice**. We either choose to pray to him or not. **Prayer is also man turning his pillows into pillars**. What this simply means is that, whilst people are asleep on their pillows at night, a man of prayer in such hours prevails and seeks for divine direction and intervention. It is sacrificing a bit of sleep for revelation truth (pillars). **Patrick M Morley (1992, p 147)**, author of ***Walking with Christ in the Details of Life***, said this about prayer and I quote, **"It is the medium of exchange between needy people and a rich God. The man who is poor in relationships, destitute in hope, and hungry for**

significance can purchase them with prayer." In this definition, Patrick defines for the purpose of an ordinary person who desires an extraordinary life. He is a needy person, hopeless, and hungry for significance. The key to unlock these natural dispositions are only through prayer, and this is exactly what we observe in the life of the Servant in context.

In **verse 12,** when the man did not know what to do, he chose to pray. He said, "**Oh *God please help me to accomplish the purpose of my journey***". Your journey to your destination in life can only be pursued with prayer. This simply calls on us to call on God when we do not know what to do. One thing we realise about this servant is that he did know his purpose but he did not know how to execute it. His purpose and mission was to find a wife but he did not know how to fulfil it. In the same way, many people have an idea of what to do but do not really know where to begin. In such situations choose to pray. Purpose makes you pray more than the ordinary. Call on the Father and He will answer. Prayer gives you the chance to see what seems hidden from you and for you. It gives you the chance to deeply understand the whys and what's you are doing in life since your Creator knows you from inside out.

❖ **The second thing** purpose makes you do is to **UNITE** or **understand** with God. A man of purpose, when he prays, also creates a sense of unity and understanding with God. Your prayer itself is a sense of unity with God.

> Be a man of superior power of discernment or enlightened intelligence.

Matthew 18:18 (NLT) says, **"What you prohibit on earth is prohibited in heaven and whatever you allow on earth is allowed in heaven."** This piece really brings about the meaning of unity with your purpose in God. **'To unite'** here means **'to join, combine, or incorporate to form a single whole or unit'**. To explain it further: You think as one with your Creator and you understand His mind which is His purpose for you. In addition, remember **Proverbs 25:5, "It is only a man of understanding who will draw his purpose near to himself."** You need to build intimacy with God so that you can understand His thinking. 'Understanding' here means **'a man of superior power of discernment or enlightened intelligence'**. In short, a man of purpose seeks unity with his Maker by becoming one with Him in order to have a superior power or knowledge of what He does not know or understand because prayer without understanding is usually ineffective. As we can notice with this servant story, his purpose further united him with God so that he could really understand the purpose of his journey.

The third thing purpose makes you do is **RISK.** **'To risk'** is **'to venture upon, take or run the chance of something'**. It is also 'the hazard or chance of loss'. They are the very things that look foolish and ridiculous to the majority. This is how purpose sometimes makes you do. Most people are not living their purpose because

> The man who is afraid to take risk usually stays at the same place for more than usual.

they are afraid to take chances. Well let me tell you, it is risky not to take risk. The man who is afraid to take risk usually stays at the same place for more than usual. It is either you risk or stay at what seems like your comfort zone. In **verse 14,** we see an example of the risk the servant took. He said, *"**Lord this is my request / risk. I will ask one of these girls for a drink. If she says, 'Yes, certainly and I will water your camels too', let it be the one you have appointed to Isaac to marry.**"* The risk was not a woman offering him water to drink. The risk was a woman going forward to serve his camel too. For a woman to give you a drink of water can be considered as normal but for her to go down and give a donkey water is something few women will do because it sounds foolish, ridiculous and insulting. Probably eight out of ten girls may either not do this or give you the worst insult of your life. This is what *risk* looks like and most of us would not have done what the servant did. It looks foolish. We stand the chance of a loss, so most of us would not even venture upon it. Nevertheless, the truth of the matter is that all the successful people you see in our streets and in life have one way or other taken chances that seems foolish and ridiculous to the majority, taken an opportunity that can lead to loss of money or some sort of investment in life. This can lead to a double size of what you already have. It is simply risky not to take a risk. Even if your risk in life does not materialise, you do not lose out, you rather learn new and better ways to pursue your purpose in life. **Thomas Edison,** the man who invented light bulbs, had to fail a thousand times before he could invent a light bulb. At the end when asked about all the risk he took before reaching his purpose, he said he had, **"at least, learnt a thousand ways of not producing a light bulb."** Likewise, it was not until the servant had taken this risk that he met Rebekah. It was his purpose to find a good wife that caused him to take such a risk. In the same way your purpose in life whether to influence people, start a dream business of your own or to start a career etc, you should be ready to take chances and venture upon things. So be all you can be by doing the things that most people will not do. Sometimes the risk will be studying at night when most people are asleep. I liked something about President Barack Obama when he was interviewed once on a news channel. He was asked how he was able to combine his busy scheduled as a presidential aspirant with his book writing, and especially making time for family activities with wife and kids. He said something most of us will not do. Obama called himself a **NIGHT OWL** explaining how, after campaigning, he would see to his wife and children and while all of them went to sleep, he would wake up again at night and sit down to write his books. That is how, even in his busy schedule, we still see his books on shelves selling. The truth is, he is doing something most of us are not doing and so getting something most of us are not getting, which is success. The risk is to go beyond a limitation or a final point. For instance, the limitation is everybody sleeping at night and going beyond is staying over to get what those who are sleeping will not get. This is risk taking.

❖ OBSERVATION:

The next key we look at is **OBSERVATION**. A principal key in a purposeful person's life is observation. To observe is to see. To deepen it, it is also necessary to recognise or identify what you see because there may be times you will see something but not recognise it. It may also mean 'to watch or look'. Everyone observes in a way that is ordinary but to go beyond just looking one has to recognise and understand what he sees. Purpose makes one to see more than the ordinary. A personal question I throw out to you is: **"What do you see in your life in the next five years?"** HOW YOU SEE DETERMINES HOW YOU STEP! If you see little, you step little but when you see big, though your now moment may be small, your end moment will be big. Moreover, remember the steps we take in life are the focal point in this book. Purpose, as defined in **chapter 1**, says that it is the steps we take to meet what we see **(vision)** and to arrive at our destination **(destiny).** In between where you are now and where you have to be is a gap. To close this gap of life, one needs to take steps (purpose). Imagine taking steps with your eyes closed .You either miss the right way or hit something and fall down. This is what happens when in our lives we live without observing or looking.

The encounter between Elijah and Elisha draws to us some lessons about been observant and focusing on what you see but before we concentrate on the perspective of the story; let us learn something from these two great men. In **2 Kings2:1-17** we learn that Elisha identified his purpose. His purpose was to get a double portion of the spirit of Elijah but to reach his purpose Elisha had to follow Elijah from Gilgal to the River Jordan, which was very far. Along the way, four times, people tried to confuse Elisha from reaching his purpose but he kept his eyes on the source of his purpose (two times by Elijah himself and twice by the prophets in those periods). This is just to show you that the road of purpose is always not easy. In **verse 10,** it is important to establish that for Elisha's request to be fulfilled he had to **see Elijah go**. Elijah said, "*If you see me when I am taking away, then you will get it but if not then you will not*". The big questions here are:

- Why did Elijah make such a profound statement? "**If you see me go when I am taking away, then you will get it.**"

- What is so important about seeing (observation) in relation to reaching your calling in life?

Elijah made such a profound statement I believe to show Elisha that *there is always a co-relation between what you see and reaching your purpose because the direction you see will always determine the steps you take to get there and that when you see clearly you can avoid unnecessary mistakes you usually make along the purpose route.*

Decisions decide life and positioning, planning and prioritizing are vital to realizing our purpose in life.

Therefore, it continued, that as they were walking and talking, suddenly, a chariot of fire appeared, drawn by horses of fire. It drove between them, separating them, and

ALIVE FOR A PURPOSE

Elijah was carried by a whirlwind into heaven. Elisha saw it and cried out, "My father, my father; the chariots of fire!" So, as they disappeared, he walked and picked up the cloak of his master Elijah's cloak and he had a double portion.

Note here that what he saw determined his steps to take what contained his purpose. Imagine if he had not seen his master go. He would not have seen the location of his cloth meaning he would have died with his music still unsung. **We are all born with music on our lips but most of us die without singing our song.**

Before we look at the servant, I want to consider an encounter between God and Abraham. In **Genesis 13:1-14** (emphasis made), we read that an argument broke between the herdsmen of Abraham and that of his nephew, Lot. To avoid this argument and a possible separation between family members, Abraham called his nephew, Lot, and talked it over with him; to observe the land and take his choice of any section he wanted.

> **In life refusing to see in a direction is also refusing to take that direction."**

In **verse 10, "Lot took a long look at the fertile plains of the Jordan valley in the direction of Zoar. The whole area was well watered, like the garden of the Lord or the beautiful land of Egypt** (This was before the Lord had destroyed Sodom and Gomorrah). **So Lot made his observation, chose this land, and went to live there."**

After Lot has made his choice, it was time for Abraham also to handpick. In **verse 14**, after Lot was gone, the Lord said to Abram, **"Look as far as you can see in every direction."** In **verse 17: "Take a walk in every direction and explore the new possessions I am giving you."**

There are two levels of observation (looking) we can identify between Abram and Lot, and as you learn the characteristics of an on-purpose person, it is important to get it right. A man of purpose observes more than the ordinary and if we are looking to observe the things around us then we have to see more than Lot saw. Even though Lot observed before choosing, we can see that:

1. Lot's observation was that of one direction and physical pleasure seeking

The Bible says that he took a long look and not a wide one. Not only did he not involve God in his selections, he also looked at one direction, which was the beautiful plains of the Jordan valley that later brought him so much trouble (his wife even turned to a pillar of salt). The ordinary observation in our life is when we allow our flesh to lead us into our choice of things we want to pursue only, but in most cases, just like Psychologist Sigmund Freud said, **"The flesh operates under the pleasure principle,"** meaning it always seeks pleasure and avoids pain. This is what happened to Lot and this is what happens to most of us. This usually happens when we pursue an ambition, career or something worthwhile in life which though we see, may not be what God wants us to do.

2. Wide observation and godly influence

When we look at Abraham, we realise something more than the ordinary. God influenced Abraham's observation and selection of where he ought to select. Secondly, Abram did not just take a long look; he took a wide look as well. He looked at every direction of the environment that was about to shape his destiny. This gave him a clearer picture of what he wanted out of life. As mentioned in **chapter 1** of this book, there is more than one thing we all can do about the ambitions and the visions but we need to be very careful about the abilities we see in our lives and the selections we make.

> "Beneath every living life is a motive, reaction and a truth that needs to be discovered."

Observe with your eyes and let your ears understand. As we turn our imagination back to the servant, we learn in **verse 15 of Genesis 24** that, as the man positioned himself at a strategic place, something happened. As he was still praying, Rebekah came with her jug to fetch water and he **saw** her. It is important to note here that God sometimes answer our prayers through surveillance, so in verse 45 the servant narrated his story by saying, **"*Before I had finished praying I saw Rebekah"*.** God avails and man prevails. Your reason for being has been made available to you and you must prevail against all odds to make it happen. In **Hebrews 11:39-40 (NLT),** God makes it clear to us that, "***He has planned so many things for us but only together with us will those things be made perfect***."

If you are one who gives up quickly you will never make real the things God has made available in your life. In life when you have seen little, you do little. So like the purposeful people we have seen in this chapter, begin to take a wide look and not just a long look at the things within and around you. Be impressed and interested in your life rather than interesting and impressive, for this is what a man of purpose operates.

❖ <u>**Searching**</u>

In the previous chapter, I explained the concept of searching using **Proverbs 25:2** again, **"It is the glory of God to conceal, it is the glory of man to search out."**

When you encounter a man on purpose, another extraordinary thing about him is the searching mentality. He searches more than the ordinary. Whoever you are born, whatever you can be has been hidden for you and not from you. All that you need to do is to add searching to prayer, understand the matter, risk in life, plan and prioritise your life, and observe the lives of purposeful people you can identify with. **"To search,"** is **"to look through your life carefully and others lives to find something missing or concealed."** It is to examine carefully in other to discover. Beneath every living life is a motive, reaction and a truth that needs to be discovered. To uncover the truth and motive about your life, calls for a searching mentality. **Searching is about adding value to the dot**.

The dot is the point we all start from but as we search beyond that point, we find that our value increases. Look at the servant. He went with nothing but came back with Rebekah. **What made the difference?** He searched for Rebekah, thereby adding value to his mission. One thing about searching is patience: a must-have virtue. We all want to succeed in life but ask yourself: **"Do you have the patience?"** This is what separates ordinary people from extraordinary ones. I believe it took some time for the servant to even locate the well and he had to endure some form of abuse from some of the women that came along. In all this, he endured and searched out his purpose. For many of us, when we search a while and do not find, we give up. The qualities of a man on-purpose are perseverance and determination to search, to find his calling and live it out. It is commonly said, **"Winners never quit, quitters never win but perseverance conquers them all"**. Three times Elijah told Elisha to stop following him but he refused until he had received what he was searching for from him. So keep examining and exploring until you have discovered the joy of the new.

❖   **Expectation**

A man was sent out on a purpose. His purpose was to find a wife for his master's son. When he had gotten to his mission field, he realised that his mission was difficult and well beyond him, but he responded more than the ordinary person would normally do. The ordinary would have abandoned his mission and returned to his master with his purpose unfulfilled but this man persevered and stayed on purpose. He realised that the key to understanding purpose was in the mind of the Creator so as read he prayed. His prayer was **Genesis 29:12, "God help me to accomplish the purpose of my journey."**

This is something most people forget in times when purpose seems lost. How many times have you sought God or counsel about a dream or a calling you want to live out? As he prayed, he built unity and understanding of what he was out there to do. Building strength and courage came from prayer to his Maker that gave him the wisdom to take risky decisions by positioning himself in line with his calling. Decisions decide life and positioning. Planning and prioritising are vital to realising our purpose in life. To get the right woman, he positioned himself by a well where mostly women were coming to draw water. Many of us expect the best out of life but we usually find ourselves in the wrong direction. As **David Thoreau** said, "**If a man advances confidently in the direction of his dreams to live the life he has imagined, he will meet with a success unexpected in common hours.**" As we have already seen in detail, he kept on searching with a positive frame of mind, with a motive of reaching his mission. The psalmist was right when he said in **Psalm 5:3**; that "**after you have done everything you wait expectantly for answers**". The results of his act led him to expect a positive result and that was finding Rebekah. Expectation is the point where confidence, faith and hope work for you. It is a point where nothing comes to prevent you reaching your purpose. It is also the point where purpose takes chances, and anticipation and

> **Expectation is the point where purpose takes chances and anticipation and endurance produce results.**

endurance produce results. There are two levels of expectation in life.

The first is **anticipating positive results out of a situation**. In **Genesis 24:23** we learn that, after the servant had fulfilled all the requirement of the servant's prayer and action, he gave her a gold ring for her nose and two large bracelets for her wrist: a symbol of engagement in those time. The point I am drawing here is that Eliezer, the servant, at that point of his journey expected the woman who would lower her jug down to serve his donkey to be the woman he had prayed for.

The second level is **expecting opposition to your purpose**. Family and friends will sometimes not support your dreams. There are problems on the route to reaching your goal. Expect them along the way. As long as you understand that, you will not let them stand in your way. Eliezer, on his mission, also expected problems. I do not personally think that most women who passed by the well that day lowered their pots to draw water to satisfy a camel that needed about thirty five gallons of water to drink after a week's travel. Paul Harvey said, "**You can always tell when you are on the road to success. It's uphill all the way**". However, in all this still have a dream and expect in faith and hope. Adversity and crisis are not our enemies. They are mirrors of success. Someone said, "*Cripple a man and you have Sir Walter Scott. Lock him in prison and you have John Bunyan. Bury him in snow of valley and you have Abraham Lincoln. Smile down on him with infantile paralysis and he becomes Franklin Delano Roosevelt. Burn him so severely that doctor's says he will not walk again and have Glen Cunningham who won the world's record, in 1934, for the one minute mile. Call him a slow learner,* *retarded, and write him off as uneducatable, and you have Albert Einstein"* (author unknown). These are men whose downfalls never hindered them from reaching a higher calling in life. You can also live your purpose even in adversity. Let your eyes continue to shine with expectations and wait upon the Lord.

Later on in the book, we will continue the story of this man and what he did next with what he found.

KEY LESSONS AND PRINCIPLES

➤ Life begins with questions, continues with questions and ends with questions.

➤ Prayer is the key to unlocking every activity on the earth, including purpose.

➤ Purpose seeks unity with your Maker in order to have a superior power or knowledge of what is not understood.

➤ How you see in life determines how you step. If you see little, you step little but when you see big, you see big and though your beginning may be small, your end will definitely be big.

➤ In life, refusing to see a direction is refusing to take it.

➤ Beneath every living life are a motive, reaction and truth that need to be discovered by having a searching mentality.

CHAPTER 5
MISSING PURPOSE

"Compared with what we ought to be, we are only half awake" (WILLIAM JASEL)

This part of the book is also very important because of the reality we are facing in the world today. From industrialised nations to third world countries, the world has become an incubator of stress, frustration, depression, futility and emptiness. The main symptom is purposelessness. It seems what historians say is right: the value of life decreases and the quality of existence diminishes when a generation loses its sense of destiny and purpose. This chapter, therefore, not only reveals the reality but also seeks to encourage you to fully wake up. For God did not create you to miss or fail in your purpose.

> **The value of life decreases and the quality of existence diminishes when a generation loses its sense of destiny and purpose**

Missing purpose is failing to live out your calling in life but the good thing is that as long as you are part of the living there is nothing like failure because failure is not final as most of us view it.

I was deeply moved by an article in the January 5, 2009 edition of the **Metro Newspaper** in the UK, which read, *"Life is meaningless for one in ten young people."*

They believe life is not worth living or has little or no purpose. Those who tend to feel this way are mainly the sixteen to twenty five year olds who are not in school, work or training. More than a quarter of those polled were depressed and stressed and less happy than when they were younger.

Though relationships with family and friends were found to be the key levels of happiness, as well as money and work, I strongly believe that there is more to these.

In another study, at a U.S university, when sixty students were asked why they had attempted suicide, 85% said the reason had been because **"life seemed meaningless."** More importantly however, was that 93% of these students who suffered from the apparent lack of purpose in their lives were socially active, achieving academically and on good terms with their families **(Richard J. Leider 2007, p 34).**

We can have means to live but no meaning to live for

Looking at these two researches conducted, we can conclude that the dream of just improving the socio-economic status of people is not enough. So whether you are in college or out of college, rich, poor, developed, or third world country, you need purpose to survive.

The word **'miss'** is **'to fail'**. It is to fail to hit a target or to take an advantage or to perceive or understand your reason for being. When this happens, we rust out because life becomes meaningless and purposeless. This feeling of emptiness and internal failure is because of:

1. Failure to connect with our maker

Purpose is inbuilt and it needs to be activated. Sometimes it naturally activates itself but mostly man has to communicate with the Creator Himself to release it. Unfortunately, the gap between man and God has been broken. We claim to know Him but our hearts are far away from His. Today's generation rather relies on its intellect, job and money and has completely ignored Him. We do not live in-purpose anymore. We live in daily hustle and bustle where man's own effort, determination, and staffs own confidence in themselves and their own power and human achievement has become the order of the day. No wonder our streets and homes are filled with stress and futility, vanity and suicide. **"For without me you can do nothing,"** Jesus said, **(John 15:5).** Moreover, this is true because we are perishing as we rely on our own strength.

Understanding purpose and living it out requires insights more than mere human wisdom.

"Many of us have become so busy and hurried so sink in our troubles and trivialities. We lose the heart to heart intimacy with Gods presence that He intends. We miss the care of joy His love can create in our lives, the way it heals our broken place and pulls us towards wholeness. Instead our lives fill up with longer and empty pockets" (Sue Monk Kidd).

2.Change in worldview

The generation of our time, especially the youth, has a wrong perception of life. Our expectation in life is to get whatever we want without much effort. When we do not get what we want, we give up. A young girl went with her dad to take piano lessons. The piano tutor lectured her on the commitment she needed to put if she wanted to become a successful pianist. When the young girl heard of the commitment she would have to make in order to make success, she gave up on it. No wonder one out of ten young people are crying aloud that life is meaningless. In today's world, we lack perseverance, consistency and the driving force we need to pursue careers and goals and our God given talents.

3.Faulty path and self-reliance

In **Jeremiah 6:16,** this is what the Lord says, "**Stand at the crossroad and look. Ask where the ancient path is, ask where the good way is and walk in it and you will find rest for your soul. But you said, 'We will not walk in it'."**

This is God's solution to a world of purposelessness but our answers have been, **"No, we will not walk in it."** The ancient path is the way that will lead us to reaching our destiny. It is the tried and tested path. It is the path that leads to discovering the joy of the new and the drive to achieve it but our answer has been, **"No, we will not walk in it."** Rather we have become self reliant individuals seeking to do things in our own wisdom, strength and riches. We glory in our own achievements and exult in our own wickedness. Our disobedience has contributed to this peril of purpose. In **Jeremiah 9:23-24,** God continues to show us the ancient path.

"**Let not the wise man boast in his wisdom or the strong man boast of his strength or the rich man boast of his riches but let him who boasts, boast about this, that he understand and knows me, that I am the Lord, who**

exercises kindness, justice and righteousness on earth, for in these delight.

Wisdom, strength and riches: In these three words, God has summed up the very things that have contributed to rust-out syndrome in our individual lives and the world as a whole. Let not anyone get me wrong. Yes, Solomon the wisest man on earth put wisdom on top of his list and strength and riches followed. Nevertheless, to this man, the fear of the Lord was the beginning of wisdom. Can so be said of our generation? What do we consider wise in our time. Is it not being akin to bullying, scheming and planning to destroy? **Dr Myles Munroe (1992)** said, "**When purpose of a thing is not known, abuse is inevitable.**"

We are abusing the very way we can achieve our purpose and this explains why many of us are failing to live purposeful lives. We live in a generation that chooses to rely on human wisdom rather than God's divine wisdom, making it difficult to possess strength and prosperity. As you continue to read the pages of this book, you will discover the importance of God's divine wisdom and purpose but for now, we fail because we rely on our own wisdom, which is usually not enough to sustain purpose. Understanding purpose and living it out requires insight more than mere human wisdom and insight.

4. Ignorance

Ignorance can be said to be our number one enemy today. The Hebrew meaning for 'ignorance' means *'darkness'*. Satan is also the 'prince of darkness' meaning he is the ruler of every area of your ignorance. So when Hosea 4:6 (KJV)says, "*My people are destroyed for lack of knowledge: because thou has rejected knowledge, I will also reject thee, that thou shalt be no priest to me: seeing thou hast forgotten the law of thy God, I will also forget thy children.,"* do not doubt because Satan fears you when you gain *revelation* knowledge. The term **'ignorance'** is the **"condition of being uneducated, unaware, or uninformed"**. It is also, **"a wilful neglect or refusal to acquire knowledge, which one may acquire, and his duty to have" (Book of Common Prayer).**

These definitions speak of two different ways about ignorance: ignorance because of not being aware or uninformed of a situation or circumstance and ignorance because of our own wilful neglect and choices; this being the most dangerous. I believe this forms a bigger proportion compared to the former. Today people are wilfully ignorant of God, resulting in ignorance in themselves and the very things they can do. We know that there is God but we refuse to acknowledge His presence. Yes, you may have been born uneducated or uninformed about the very important things in life but as you grow, you have the choice to search and find. We live in an information age and there is no excuse for being ignorant in the very things that matter to our lives. **Maya Angelou, (US author and poet in 1928)** said, **"We allow our ignorance to prevail upon us and make us think we can survive alone, alone in patches, alone in groups, alone in races, even alone in genders".** This is why our generation is **rusting out**.

> Today people are wilfully ignorant of God, resulting in ignorance in themselves and the very things they can do

"Nothing in the entire world is more dangerous than sincere ignorance and conscientious stupidity". Martin Luther King Jr. (Strength of Love, 1963). We think we know it all but we do not. We think we have seen it all but we have seen nothing. What this generation is rather doing is exposing it's self to the danger of dying without fulfilling our purpose in life. This is how God sees our generation today.

"And the people served the Lord all the days of Joshua, and all the days of the elders who outlived Joshua, who had seen all the great work that the Lord had done for Israel. And Joshua, the son of Nun, the servant of the Lord, died at the age of 110 years... and all that generation also were gathered to their fathers. And there arose another generation after them who did not know the Lord or the work that he had done for Israel. And the people of Israel did what was evil in the sight of the Lord and served the Baals. And they abandoned the Lord, the God of their fathers, who had brought them out of the land of Egypt. They went after other gods, from among the gods of the peoples who were around them and bowed down to them. And they provoked the Lord to anger" Judges 2:7-12 (ESV).

Our ancestors knew God so they did not see life as meaningless, as we do today. They lived purposeful lives and enjoyed all the days of their lives. Now is our time but we have neglected the Giver of life and purpose and this is greatly affecting us.

5. Lack of understanding of vision, mission, destiny, value and purpose.

I believe most people have given up on purpose because they lack the true meaning of vision, destiny, value and purpose. When we drift away from the meaning of these, it causes confusion. That is why, in **Chapter 1,** I took my time to explain in bits what these are and the differences between them. Knowing them puts you in a stronger position about what you are doing in your life. Most people cannot differentiate their vision from their mission or ambition or any of them. When we take them for granted we, in turn, suffer the consequences. Just like it is said above, ignorance is not an excuse. You need to do your best to understand who you are. If not, you will suffer.

6. Moving around with the wrong friends, company or environment

Today, most people fail because of the wrong company they keep. Being around people, who do not believe in purpose, will only result in the failure of your calling! You need to be around people who speak with understanding of not exiting with nothing, people who will create the idea of purpose and fulfilment of destiny. Stop connecting with people who do not believe in the bigger picture God has for you. These people are a point of contact to failures because they do not add up to your life.

All his life, the young man, Jacob, had been known as a deceiver. Even at birth, he held onto the foot of his senior brother because he wanted to be born first. Growing up in an environment where his mother manipulated him to cheat his father and brother by receiving the first born blessing, he ran away to stay with his uncle who was even more of a twister and a deceiver than his former environment. This young man never met his purpose in life until one day he took his family and left his uncle's environment. On his way, he had a desperate moment and sent his family ahead of him because the next day, Esau, his elder brother, whom he cheated, was coming to meet him. Whilst on their way, he had a night with God and an angel of the Lord visited him. They wrestled all night until morning. The word of God says he wrestled until the angel wanted to go. Sensing the determination of the young man, the angel asked of his name, which he changed. He gave him the name, Israel, meaning 'prince with God'. This became the new destiny and purpose of a man who was known as the deceiver.

Note that it was the change of environment and friends that helped him to discover himself. In the same way, as long as you keep to those friends who fail to speak about the idea of purpose and Gods plan for your life, you are bound to failure.

7. Pursuing wrong purposes in life

One of the mistakes many people make is living deluded lives: lives that seem to be focusing on purpose but actually are not. The fact that what you are doing seems to have the characteristics of purpose, achieving life does not actually mean that you are living on-purpose lives. As you study what purpose is, it is also important that you also understand what purpose is NOT because we often fail by following defected or broken purposes in life. This is what I mean:

❖ **Purpose is not a wishful thinking:**

In chapter 1, I have already said much about this point. The truth is that wishes are feelings and we are not our feelings. For instance, the fact that you just see a nice car, and you wish for one, does not immediately get you that car. It is what you do after that can bring you that dream car. What wishes alone do is to create a form of destructive element to your purpose. Until you develop a plan, set priorities and develop a determined and committed mindset, you will keep hoping that things will work and happen, just like the Melito story, in chapter 1.

❖   Purpose is not your six to six kind of work (death):

Are you that kind of person who wakes up in the morning, puts on your shirt and tie, and goes to the office or your job place, to solely make money or profit? If you are, then you are mistaken. God's purpose for your life goes beyond that. This explains why you still come

> **Getting around people who do not believe in purpose will only result in failure of your calling**

back home feeling unhappy about yourself and complaining about how your job is killing you. You work for a boss you never like and receive salary below your own expectation. I am speaking about the kind of job that may grant you a means of living but do you have a meaning to live for? The truth is, when you are living Gods purpose for your life, work ceases to be a six to six kind of death but a six to six kind of living, where you love what you do and do what you love.

❖   Purpose is not manipulating people.

You may still feel you are living on-purpose life even if what you do is to manipulate people. You are actually failing God. Ask yourself:

1. Is what I am doing benefiting people or hindering people from progress?

2. Do I have people's best interest at heart or am I just in for the taking?

If your answer to any of these is **"Yes",** then you are failing God and your purpose. The purpose of this book encourages you to stop manipulating people and start motivating people. There is a thin line between these two so do not miss your purpose by manipulating.

❖ **Purpose is mostly not in your appointment:**

Here, most people are easily mistaken by taking your latest appointment to be your purpose. Whilst this may be true, however, your purpose in life very often is in your disappointment. Study biblical characters like Abraham, Joseph, David and others. You will understand where your purpose can come from. Even in our generation today, study the lives of Joni, Jessica Cox and my dad. All of their stories have been shared in this book. One thing unique about them is how they discovered their God given purpose. It was through their disappointments. Crisis is your mirror of purpose.

❖ **Purpose is not your destiny:**

A majority of people fail on-purpose because it is easy to follow destiny and forget purpose. One thing you should understand is that purpose is really the journey to your destiny. In **chapter 1**, I explained, through the Bible, that your destiny is who you are born to be whilst your purpose is the day-to-day steps you take to get to who you will be. This is what makes purpose the journey. The mistake people often make is focussing on getting to the destination and forgetting the route to the desired life. This is what author **John Maxwell** referred to as **"destination disease".** One must learn to enjoy the journey (purpose) as much as the destination (destiny).

❖ <u>**Purpose is not looking for backdoors when things become rough.**</u>

Most people give up quickly on purpose, forgetting that the purpose route is filled with diverse challenges. If you are that kind of person who gives up so quickly, then you will fail at fulfilling your God given purpose. Real purpose involves operating on a no exit strategy once you have discovered who you are. You need the right attitude to achieve significance in life, not take backdoors when things become rough.

8. **People fail when they focus on their weakness rather than strength.**

In the life of every living being, there are areas in life you cannot do much about and, on the other hand, there are areas of strength you can enlarge to fulfil purpose. The problem today is that the majority of us focus and worry our efforts on weaknesses about us and others rather than enlarging those that can yield results. *Consider a person for instance who is naturally gifted and talented in interior designing but is currently struggling to become an accountant.* Though such a person might become an accountant at the end, it is also very likely such a person will become a frustrated and confused accountant. The truth is, you can become a reactive person where the negative conditions and circumstances you face in life and the environment affects what you can and have been born to do. When you are a child, it is clearly true that conditions determine your decisions but as you grow to maturity, it is rather your choices that determine your conditions. This is because, as a matured person, the power to choose right even in the midst of negative and unproductive unconditional situations are in your hands. As long as you concentrate, for much of your life, on those conditions and circumstances you have less or no control about, you become a failure in life and achieve nothing except fear, frustration and a defeated mentality. **Dr Stephen R. Covey (2004, p 84)** declared that, **"as long as we are working in our circle of concern, we empower the things within them to control us. We empower what is out there to control us."**

We possess the choice and power to focus on our God given destinies, visions and creativity in the midst of victimisation or even tragedy. The biblical character, David, once returned from war and found out that invaders had raided his town and made away with the women and children. For what happened next, come with me in your imagination to **1 Samuel 30:4-6 (KJV):**

"Then David and the people that were with him lifted up their voice and wept, until they had no more power to weep. And David's two wives were taken captives, Ahinoam the Jezreelite, and Abigail the wife of Nabal the Carmelite. And David was greatly distressed; for the people spake of stoning him, because the soul of all the people was grieved, every man for his sons and for his

daughters: but David encouraged himself in the Lord his God."

Notice how the people, with David, reacted to the situation. They cried and showed an irresponsible attitude towards David. This is exactly how most of us behave when it comes to fulfilling our calling in life. We blame others for our mistakes and failures. We concentrate our time and energy on our weakness. David, on the other hand, proactively empowered himself in the Lord and at the end fulfilled his purpose by bringing his family and that of his friends back. The same situation weakened others but on the other hand empowered David.

To conclude this chapter, God has the best idea for your life. "**Why fail while you are still alive?**" You have the chance to experience life's value and significance. The best way to overturn your failure into success is to turn and face the opposite direction. Should you turn these points of missing purpose in an opposite direction, you will begin to see success. In the next chapter, I'll take you on a journey to discovering your purpose in life and experience the joy of life. As long as you are breathing on this planet, you have a purpose ready to be discovered because you are missing in action until you do.

KEY LESSONS AND PRINCIPLES

➢ Do not be deceived, you can have means to live but no meaning to live for. You need purpose to survive.

➢ The journey of discovering purpose requires a life-long connection and relationship with God your maker.

➢ If you want to achieve your calling in life, stop trying to achieve alone in groups, race or even in gender; connect with others to make it.

➢ Avoid point of contact to failures, if you want to discover and live your purpose. Unproductive friends and environments can be negative points of contact.

➢ You are missing in action until you discover and live your purpose.

CHAPTER 6
FINDING PURPOSE

Until purpose is fulfilled, existence has no meaning; for purpose is the source of fulfilment. By now, you understand what purpose is and why people fail to realise their purpose. In this chapter, you will find out how to know and begin

Finding purpose is finding your strength and living it and the more you live it the more successful you will become

to live by purpose. Finding purpose is finding your strength and living it and the more you live it the more successful you will become. The fact that most of us have missed purpose does not entirely mean that God has given up on this generation. He still loves and cares for us and those who will seek him in spirit and in truth will find Him. You are not outside the will of God. You are still in His plans. I must say that there are no definite ways of getting to know your purpose but there are guides to finding the real you and living in happiness. Through experience and exposure, I have come to appreciate the various ways purpose can be discovered.

I was in church one beautiful Sunday. During worship, the Holy Spirit whispered in my heart that I was going to have a call immediately after church. I received that in good faith because I was personally waiting for an important document I had been praying and waiting on God for. The biblical phrase, **"for I know the plans I have for you,"** is true because it's only God who knows the plan He has for us. Most of the time what we think is God's plan for our lives may not be that. Here I was thinking the call I was going to get after church would be concerning the document I so badly desired. I remember after church while I walked home, I held tightly to my Nokia phone determined not to miss that call the Holy Spirit had whispered to my heart.

On my way, something happened. I wore a jean trouser and a long-sleeved top and held no Bible that day. I had walked about a mile when suddenly someone driving in a car blew his horn on me. I turned back and there came from the car a medium built young white man. I wondered why he had stopped me. I remember he first asked my name and I replied by asking his. "Chris," he said. He asked me where I originated from and when I said where, he started speaking my language back to me. I started to laugh but to my surprise he spoke in about five international languages at that very moment.

I was shocked, not because it was not possible for a man to do that but because of the circumstance at the time. He spoke straight to me that I was coming from church and yes I was but judging from my clothes very few people could identify that. I was getting intrigued at this point. Then, he told me that he had gone out of his route and followed me just to tell me something. In his own

"Knowing your purpose in life, growing to your maximum potential in life, and sowing seeds that benefit others."
John Maxwell

words he said, **"Please help revive this nation."** After he had said that, he sat in his car turned back and in a matter of seconds, I could not trace his whereabouts until today. When I had taken about three steps, the Holy Spirit again whispered strongly in my heart with this exact word. "This is the call I told you about in the morning. Take it from me, you did not meet Chris, you have met Christ."

Since this meeting, I have found my purpose. Today my purpose is to revive, restore and refresh people to have hope and live the kind of life God has for them no matter the difficulty and stress we face. Since then God has put me in the process to the promise. I find myself writing and teaching people to be encouraged and not give up in life. I now speak in places I only dreamt about and do things that are in line with my purpose. You can do the same, you can find your calling and you can be successful. **John Maxwell (2008, p58)** zeroed in on the definition of success. No matter whom people are or what they want to do you should **"know your purpose in life, growing to your maximum potential in life and sowing seeds that benefit others."**

Therefore, I encourage you to get to know your purpose in life by:

1.   **Getting back to the source (Creator)**

One of the reasons our world is rusting out of purpose is because we have neglected the ancient path. The Creator of the universe holds your life in His hands. You have the choice to do whatever you like with your life but the truth is it is an option you do not have to take.

ALIVE FOR A PURPOSE

God is a God of purpose and the source of your calling. He made everything in this world out of invisible things we do not see so you will know who you are, what to do with your life and why you have been born to get back to His path.

In **Jeremiah 29:11 (KJV),** God spoke to a generation in exile. Those same circumstances represent in us a generation of people who are captives of meaningless lives and emptiness hopes. **"For I know the thoughts that I think toward you, saith the Lord, thoughts of peace, and not of evil, to give you an expected end."**

In **Jeremiah 1:5,** He knows you before you were even formed in your mother's womth; that your birth is for a reason and in Him lays your fulfilment. When Jeremiah got to know his Creator, he made a profound statement that we all need to uphold. In **Jeremiah 10:23 (NLT)** he said, **"I know Lord that a person's life is not his own. No one is able to plan his own course."**

To the creative person, ideas become original and expressive

Your destiny lives you; you do not live your destiny. Instead of wasting time in areas you do not pose strength in, it is better to recognise the presence of God in your life because your life is not your own and planning your own course is not your job. God's ability to direct your life is far superior to yours. Jeremiah also teaches us that purpose is universal. The universality of purpose only needs to be activated by you and the only way to get to activate your purpose is to turn on the Spirit of God in you. **1 Cor. 2:12 (KJV)** says:

ALIVE FOR A PURPOSE
"Now we have received, not the spirit of the world, but the spirit which is of God; that we might know the things that are freely given to us of God."

Your purpose is universal and it is free but it needs to be activated. The only way you can is to make active the God spirit in you. For just us the flesh only gives birth to flesh so the spirit reveals what God has for you from the spiritual perspective. **Who are we to question and doubt God when it comes to the purpose of man?** Doubting God's power, presence, sovereignty, wisdom, and authority is risking your purpose. In **Job 38 – 40,** Job out of ignorance, questioned God's purpose for his life. God responded with questions Job could not answer.

He has a purpose for you but remember that they may unfold over the course of your life. So do not doubt Him, rather get to know Him. Let not fear sway you from His power and presence. Let God correct your plans and give you wisdom to your calling. For what God calls you for, He also provides for.

2. Discover Yourself

Discovery is the power of purpose. To discover is simply to uncover what is covered. To find your purpose in life you should learn to uncover what God has covered for your life. In **chapter 3**, much has been said about discovery and how important it is to find your purpose. It is God's glory to hide things. That is what simply makes Him God over the earth. Whatever is valuable is hidden for man to discover- gold, oil, bauxite. Even tables are hidden in trees! It is not until a tree is cut down and sapped that beautiful dining tables and chairs are made and seen. On the other hand, what makes man glorious is in having the ability to discover what is covered. As we see, life is like a puzzle, a riddle and a quest and we in turn make the effort to fix, explain and search for the matter.

The key to purpose is to start with discovering what is needed and wanted and producing right where you are. It starts with the little ideas that come to your mind. Gaining ideas of the patterns of life is what it means to be human.

Discovery comes through different ways and forms. We:

❖   **Discover through creativity.**

❖   **Discover our talents and gifts.**

❖   **Discover solitude.**

❖   **Discover through listening to our hearts.**

1.   Discover through creativity: creativity is the central source of meaning in our lives. For most of the things that are interesting and important in our lives are because of creativity. To the creative person, ideas become original and expressive. In his book *"The Power of Purpose"*, **Richard Lieder (1997, p26)** asserted, **"Purpose is the creative positive spirit of life moving through us from inside out"**.

God is a God of purpose and the source of your calling

What Richard means is that creativity lives inside of you and it takes a positive spirit to live it out and that positive spirit is the Spirit of God that created you. In **Genesis 2:7**, since we are made in Gods created image, we also have the power to be original and progressive. Picture for a moment the nature of the earth when God first found it. It was void and without form. Out of this God created the beautiful world that we all behold. In the same way, you too can be creative. In his book **"Flow"**, psychologist, **Csikszentmlialyi Mihaly (1990)** said, **"We are happiest when we are been creative because we lose our sense of self and get the feeling that we are part of something greater. We are actually created to get satisfaction and pleasure from discovery and creativity because its results lead to our survival as species. New ideas are needed more than ever if the planet is going to survive, and the best are likely to come from genuinely creative people."**

The love of God is what makes us happy because His love begins creativity in our broken places and pulls us towards survival as species. As we relate to our environment and the very things God has created, we ignite that power within us. Everyone has the power to be creative. It starts with having the drive to work hard towards a goal. Having the sheer desire to accomplish something for yourself and your generation is the key factor to creativeness.

2.   **Discover by talent**.

Talents are the gift God has given to you. They are your natural abilities. We are all born with a gift and until we identify our talents, purpose is inevitable. **John Maxwell (2008, p59)** asserted **"people's purpose are connected to their giftedness, improvement is always related to ability."** The greater your natural abilities the greater your potential for improvement. So why try becoming something you are not while your gifts can make an easy way for you. For instance on a scale of 1-10 your gift already places you on about scale 4. With this you can, with ease and some effort, improve to a scale of 8 or 9. On the other hand, struggling in areas we are not gifted in can only lead us to an average scale. It may be good but not enough. So just like all-star Base Ball Catcher, Jim Sundberg, said, **"Discover your uniqueness, and then discipline yourself to develop it."** The question may be: I have difficulty discovering my talent, how do I find and develop it? Here are a few suggestions to help you

♣ **What are the things you do well?** Ask yourself.

Someone once said, **"This is a million dollar question only you can answer."** For instance, I find myself encouraging and reviving friends anytime they encounter any form of life difficulties. Even older people share with me their deepest secret sometimes because they trust my judgment and advice. Overtime I have identified reviving, restoring and refreshing worried souls as my natural gifts. Though I still read and study about how to motivate people, I find out that most of the things I am even learning are those I have already started doing. We all have gifts and identifying what moves you is a key to your purpose

♣ **What are the things people praise or commend you about?**

The book of Proverbs 22:9 (KJV)says, **"Seest thou a man diligent in his business? He shall stand before kings; he shall not stand before mean men"**. This simply means people

> "People's purpose are connected to their giftedness."
> John Maxwell

will observe your gift and talk about them. Your gift will always make ways for you because of how people will commend you. I have had times when people come to me and commend me for my advice because it gives peace, comfort and solutions in times when they needed them.

♣ **Identify the things you are most passionate about**: the motivation to living a purpose life must be accompanied by a burning desire.

You must be moved by passion. Passion is about been true to yourself and putting your heart into the things you identify as your purpose in life. As **Earl Nightingale** puts it **"the more intensely we feel about an idea or a goal, the more assuredly the idea buried deep in our subconscious, will direct us along the path to its fulfilment"** Personally, encouraging and motivating people is what moves me in life.

♣ **Be specific**: You may be blessed with two or more gifts but the more specific you are, the more strength you will develop.

Only you can identify the few gifts you will like to operate in. When it comes to talents, most of us think too broadly but the more specific we are the more fulfilling life becomes. **Zig Ziglar** asserted, **"You can't make it as a wondering generality."** You must become a meaningful specific. In **Luke 10-38:42**, Jesus went to visit sisters, Mary and Martha. While there Mary specifically sat at his feet to listen to his teachings but Martha wondered around doing so many things in the kitchen. When she got tired she came to Jesus and complained that Mary was only doing one specific thing, while she was trying to do everything. **Verse 41** says, **"But the Lord said to her, 'My dear Martha, you** are only so upset over all these details but there are really one thing worth been concerned about. **Mary has discovered it and I will not take it away from her.'** In these words, Jesus teaches us not be so concerned about general details but to discover the specific things in our life for in that lies our strength and purpose.

3. Listen to Your Heart:

It is said that, **"When you have a rainbow deep down in your heart, your smile will shine bright. You know you're a part of that colourful, magical, feeling you'll find when you have a rainbow inside."** How I wish that we all had a rainbow heart where we can find the rhythm to our life. In **Jeremiah 17:9,** we learn that, the heart is such that one moment it can be deceitful and desperately wicked but on the other hand, it can be very rewarding according to its actions. The state of our heart is determined by the actions we take. Charles W. Chesnutt sums it all up when he said, The workings of the human heart are the profoundest mystery of the universe. One moment they make us despair of our kind and the next we see in them the reflection of the divine image. For there to be an understanding and direction for our lives, there should be an alignment with our hearts, so when you have positively position your heart from deceit and despair, you will never go wrong by following its direction. The following points will help you to understand why you should listen to your heart.

❖ **It is the point where God examines man and man can raise himself to God.**

In **Jeremiah 17:9**, God still examines our heart and rewards its motive. Rene Daumal captured this in his piece, Mount Analogue, and I quote "**In the mythic tradition, the mountain is the bond between the earth and sky. Its solitary summit reaches the sphere of eternity, and its base spreads out in manifold foothills into the world of mortals. It is the way by which man raise himself to the divine and by which the divine reveal itself to man.**"

❖ **It is in the heart we discover good treasures**.

Jesus said in **Luke 6:45 (KJV)** "**A good man out of the good treasure of his heart bringeth forth that which is good; and an evil man out of the evil treasure of his heart bringeth forth that which is evil: for of the abundance of the heart his mouth speaketh.**" In your heart lie deep products that can preserve your life. Treasures are valuable and priceless. Our actions determine the state of our heart. The choice of your treasure will determine the end product.

❖ **It knows all things**.

The question is not what the heart knows, but rather what does not the heart knows. That is why you need to be careful the way you treat your heart, because the very important things about you may be hidden from you. Learn to live an openhearted life, pay particular attention to what your heart says to you and what you accept into it.

❖ **The heart is receptive (Rev. 3:20 (KJV))**.

ALIVE FOR A PURPOSE

"Behold, I stand at the door, and knock: if any man hear my voice, and open the door, I will come in to him, and will sup with him, and he with me". This verse is not only for new converts but also to us all. If we open the door of our hearts to God, He will come in and have fellowship with you. Imagine having communication with God. Your purpose will not elude you when He comes into your heart.

❖ **There are matters in the heart.**

I have already explained what a matter is: anything that has weight and that can occupy space. All the great things in the world come from the heart. Somebody made this simple statement, "**When the heart decides.**" I find this true because when the heart decides, the mind always accepts and out of the abundance of the heart, the mouth speaks.

4. **Being a contrarian.**

The dictionary defines **'a contrarian'** as **'a person who takes an opposing view, especially, one who rejects the majority opinion, as in economic matters'**. Now, this word is usually used for investors: the kind of investors who invest contrary to that of the majority, the reason being that he views things from a different angle. Whilst all investors are thinking in the present, they have already thought about the future. Another definition of **'a contrarian'** is **'someone who lives life backwards'**. I strongly believe that one of the ways to discover your purpose in life is to learn to be a contrarian because God is a contrarian. What do I mean?

"You saw me before I was born. Every day of my life was recorded in your book. Every moment was laid out before a single day had passed" Psalm 139:16 (NLT).

"You have decided the length of our lives. You know how many months we will live, and we are not given a minute longer" Job 14:5 (NLT).

"I knew you before I formed you in your mother's womb. Before you were born, I set you apart and appointed you as my spokesman to the world" Jeremiah 1:5 (NLT).

God is a contrarian because He views your life from backwards and not the present. In the verses above, God had finished with your life before you even began it. God knows your purpose and destiny. He knows the difficulty you will be in, your failures and success, and everything about you before you even encounter it. This explains why sometimes it is very difficult to deal with God because while you are thinking about the present, He is looking at your life from the future.

> God is a contrarian because he views your life from backwards and not the present

We can also become contrarian when we are able to use past experiences to predict our future. A contrarian begins with something they love about their life and trace it back until they find something awful that they realise has led to a great thing they love about their life now. A great example can be found in **Chapter 2**, where we shared the stories of great people. It was the diving accident in 1967 that left Joni Eareckson Tada, a quadriplegic, in a wheelchair but today this misfortune has led her to live on-purpose life by establishing Joni and Friends (JAF) in 1979, an organisation for Christian ministry in the disability community throughout the world. In the same way, my father's success can be traced back to the period he lost her wife. If not that, my father probably would not have discovered himself to help his children to reach the level we are at now.

Looking at these instances above, you can conclude that the bad things became the foundation of something better later in their lives. Bad events support good things. In life, bad things can happen to good people and good things can happen to bad people but the gift of being a contrarian is to understand that crisis is the mirror of purpose and as the Bible says in **Romans 8:28, "all things work together for good."**

5.   Maximise time.

Time is a perishable commodity. Once you lose it, you cannot get it back. It is like placing a bag of tomatoes in the centre of a high street. If it gets run over by a car, you cannot do anything with those tomatoes again. Time is also like a bank account. Every day, it credits you with 86,400 seconds. By the close of the night, it writes you off as loss whatever you fail to use to discover or put to proper use. It carries forward no balances, neither does it allow overdraft and there is no going back. Our lives are filled with *chronos* and *kairos* moments that God expects us to invest to get the most success and significance. To sum up, watch how you use your time and energy. Below are:

10 ways to maximise your time effectively:

❖ **Keep a diary**: Simply make a 'to do' list on a daily or weekly basis.

❖ **Set priorities**: Attempt the top 20% of your 'to do' list, on a daily basis. Do not attempt to do much.

❖ **Avoid procrastination**: Be self disciplined with your time. Procrastination will frustrate and affect God's purpose for your life. Do things early and on time!

❖ **Avoid perfectionism**: Perfectionist never gets things done. Pursue excellence in all you do but stop trying to be perfect.

❖ **Control interruptions**: Be careful of telephone conversations or visitors dropping in between scheduled activities. Your inability to say **"No,"** to some of these instances, can waste your time on a daily basis.

❖ **Get organised**: You can do this by constantly using a calendar. This will help you to plan and stay focussed on time.

❖ **Work can't see hours**: Seize small units of time. When travelling on a long journey, what do you do? Do you just eat on the bus or watch only movies on a flight. Those are also times for reading a book, writing a chapter, completing your 'to do' list etc

❖ **Be less aware**: Let events takes care of themselves rather than constantly peeping at the clock.

❖ **Review daily**: Always review what you have done on a daily basis. This will help your tomorrow to be better.

❖ **Listen to the Holy Spirit**: Spending quality time on a daily basis alone with the Holy Spirit is the best way to maximise your time, life and purpose. Jesus Christ woke up every morning to spend quality time with the planner of life (Holy Spirit).

In conclusion, this chapter has delved into some of the most effective ways you can discover your purpose in life and how you can do this. You are not a failure as long as you are alive. To be more proactive, look back from the last chapter and turn all the listed failures to success because just as **IBM Founder, T.J. Watson,** said, **"Success is on the far side of failure."**

KEY LESSONS AND PRINCIPLES

➤ Until purpose is fulfilled, existence has no meaning because purpose is the source of fulfilment.

➤ Discovery is the power of purpose. To discover is simply to uncover what has been covered.

➤ Since we are made in God's image, we possess the power to be original and progressive.

➤ Discover through creativity, talents and gifts, solitude and listening to your heart.

➤ Things to watch out for if you want to discover:

1. Things you love to do well.
2. Things people already praise you about.
3. Things you are mostly passionate about
4. In all these things, be specific and do not wander about.

CHAPTER SEVEN
THE BENEFITS OF PURPOSE

In this chapter, we deepen our conversation about ALIVE ON PURPOSE and the benefits of living yours to the maximum. Can there be more to life than just going to work every day doing your job? On the other hand, is there a good reason why one should look for a unique work or a job? The answer is: Yes, there is much to life than just work. The truth is, no matter our work or role in life, we should also view it as God's special calling to serve in our calling. God has a plan for your life and it is the only way to fulfilment in your life. When our lives are empty of love, peace, and joy, or when you constantly wake up in the middle of the night asking yourself who you are or whether you have the means to live but no meaning to live for, then it is a sign that you are living outside the will of God. As already established, God has specifically placed purpose in our lives for our own benefits. This explains why His plan for us stands forever in our hearts through all generations. Indeed Isaiah speaks of the benefit of God purpose for you in this way:

> No matter our work or role in life, we should also view it as God's special calling to serve

Isaiah 55:10-11 (NLT)

"The rain and snow come down from the heavens and stay on the ground to water the earth. They cause the grain to grow, producing seed for the farmer and bread for the hungry. It is the same with My word. I send it out and it always produces fruit. It will accomplish all I want it to and it will prosper everywhere I send it."

This is what God means. His purpose for your life is like rain that waters the earth. Emblematically, **water** is a blessing; this explains why when it rains to the ground it results in productivity and makes a farmer produces crops in abundance to feed the hungry. So is God's purpose for your life. We are created to grow to our full potential and to yield results. Your purpose also will lead you to accomplish and prosper in your generation. This mission represents the central piece of your life. Living in this central piece of your life is the key to inner peace and joy.

1.   **When a man discovers his calling, he also discovers the joy of something new**.

Joy is the outflow of excitement, not carved from the outside but flows naturally from inside, so when we live life from the inside out, the result is joy unspeakable:

Isaiah 55:12-13 (NLT)

"You will live in joy and peace. The mountains and hills will burst into song, and the trees of the field will clap their hands! Where once there were thorns, cypress trees will grow. Where briers grew, myrtles will sprout up. This miracle will bring great honour to the Lord's name; it will be an everlasting sign of His power and love."

The **mountains** and the **hills** here refer to the obstacles of living meaningless lives. The **briers** and **thorns** stand for the pains that come because of futility of life. Where there is purpose these things give way to joy and peace.

This feeling is different from happiness. Happiness comes because of material things but the former flows even when they are not there. Ultimate joy goes beyond riches. It is living a Christ-centred purpose life. That is why the apostle Paul, even when in prison, could admonish the church to live in joy.

In Philippians 4:4 (KJV) he said,

"Rejoice in the Lord always: *and* again I say, rejoice."

Under normal circumstances just ask yourself: How can a man in prison encourage others outside prison to rejoice? It is only because, even in prison, Paul was still living his purpose from inside out. Just like Mensa Otabil said, **"You can imprison a person but you cannot imprison his power of imagination."** Paul may have been imprisoned but he lived purpose from the inside out. Therefore, when you operate in your purpose, you reap the joy of restoring lost glories. This happened in the time of Nehemiah when he gathered the people together to hear Ezra's law:

Neh. 8:10-12 (KJV)

"You can imprison a person but you cannot imprison his power of imagination"
Mensah Otabil

"Then he said unto them, 'Go your way, eat the fat, and drink the sweet and send portions unto them for whom nothing is prepared: for *this* day *is* holy unto our Lord: neither be ye sorry; for the joy of the Lord is your strength.' So the Levites stilled all the people, saying, 'Hold your peace, for the day *is* holy; neither be ye grieved.' And all the people went their way to eat and to drink and to send portions and to make great mirth because they had understood the words that were declared unto them."

Their understanding of God's purpose for their lives restored joy back into their lives.

2. **Purpose will transform your life**.

When your life is exposed to God's original idea for you, there is a reaction and this causes transformation. When we live on-purpose lives, we reap the benefit of discovering the joy of the new. Why? Because like Napoleon Hill said,

> **When a man discovers his calling, he also discovers the joy of something new.**

"**First come thought; then organisation of that thought into ideas and plans; then transformation of those plans into reality. The beginning, as you will observe, is in your imagination.**" It is the imagination and ideas which our calling brings, that shapes and transforms us. Therefore, the Bible encourages *us, in Romans 12:2, this way:*

"*And* be not conformed to this world: but be ye transformed by the renewing of your mind, that ye may prove what is that good, and acceptable, and perfect, will of God."

It does not matter how undesirable life may be to you. As long as you stay committed to your purpose, God can change your life in just a moment:

Genesis 41:39-40 (NLT)

"Turning to Joseph, Pharaoh said, 'Since God has revealed the meaning of the dreams to you, you are the wisest man in the land! I hereby appoint you to direct this project. You will manage my household and organise all my people. Only I will have a rank higher than yours.'"

Exodus 12:36 (NLT)

"The Lord caused the Egyptians to look favourably on the Israelites and they gave the Israelites whatever they asked for. So, like a victorious army, they plundered the Egyptians!"

In these two examples, I draw your mind to how transforming the life of an individual and a whole generation can be. Joseph was sold into slavery and later thrown into prison for sins he did not commit but enduring the entire situation, he stayed committed to his calling. The very day he was called to explain the king's dream, God transformed his life. Joseph rose to the top in one day, from prison walls to Prime Minister in Pharaoh's palace. In the same way, the Israelites had been in slavery for 430 years, a population of about two million. After all these years, they stayed faithful regarding the promises of God for their lives. No wonder, in just a period of twenty four hours, God had transformed their situations.

If you are conscious of your calling though facing hard times, your life will change.

3. Purpose will create in you an understanding of, not just who you are, but what is important.

A man of understanding is a man of wisdom. It is better in your life to understand what is important than to know everything. There are specific things you have been

> **Purpose will create in you an understanding of not just who you are but what is important.**

created for. Knowing and keeping your eyes on the main things are the keys to a successful living. When there is no purpose, you become jack-of-all-trades but a master of none. You do too many things and often the wrong ones. Purpose will create in you the recipe for effective living. When we look into the life of Jesus, we see a man who from His early beginnings understood what His purpose was and how important for Him to concentrate just on it. At a tender age of twelve, He told his parents:

Luke 2:49 (NLT)

"But why did you need to search?" He asked. "You should have known that I would be in my Father's house."

He pursued only what mattered to His life and throughout His thirty three years of living He finished that purpose. The three most important aspect of his ministry can be found in:

Matthew 4:23 (NLT)

"Jesus travelled throughout Galilee, teaching in the synagogues, preaching everywhere the good news about the kingdom. And He healed people who had every kind of sickness and disease."

He thought, preached and healed. He kept His mind on the main things instead of wasting time on what He was not called to do. When we also live purposeful lives, we reap the benefit of accomplishing the task.

4. Purpose reduces fear and helps you to go beyond limitations. When you live by purpose, fear no longer becomes false evidence that appears real; rather it becomes a

> Purpose reduces fear and helps you to go beyond limitations.

necessity for courage. With purpose, a situation of fear becomes a friend, a helper, because you react positively to it.   You have not been given the spirit of fear and timidity but of power and sound mind so that you can be a winner in life. Purpose drives you forward and sustains you in areas of competitive advantage. **'A limitation'** is **'a final point or a restricted area'**. It is usually *fear* that stops you from enlarging your capacity but when you fulfil your purpose you gain the right energy to make the right decisions. You remember the story of Abraham's servant and the decision he took while on his way to search for Rebecca. He knew his purpose so took a risk that many would not take. At the end, his risk paid off and he was successful. The truth about purpose is that it leads you to accomplish your destiny. Based on this fact, you can become assured that until you have fulfilled your destiny nothing negative can affect you. This is what made David say:

Psalm 23:4 (KJV)

"Yea, though I walk through the valley of the shadow of death, I will fear no evil; for thou *art* with me; thy rod and thy staff they comfort me."

David was aware of God's intended purpose for his life so he did not entertain fear even in such situations. He rather chose to live in faith knowing that his purpose would lead him to his destiny. In the same way, Jesus demonstrated this courage while He was with His disciples:

Mark 4:34-41 (KJV)

"And the same day, when the evening was come, He saith unto them, 'Let us pass over unto the other side.' And when they had sent away the multitude, they took Him even as He was in the ship. And there were also with Him other little ships. And there arose a great storm of wind and the waves beat into the ship, so that it was now full. And He was in the hinder part of the ship, asleep on a pillow; and they awake Him, and say unto Him, 'Master, carest thou not that we perish?' And He arose; He rebuked the wind and said unto the sea, 'Peace, be still.' And the wind ceased and there was a great calm. And He said unto them, 'Why are ye so fearful? How is it that ye have no faith?' And they feared exceedingly, and said one to another, 'What manner of man is this, that even the wind and the sea obey Him?'**

Now the question I want you to think about is:

♣ Why was Jesus not afraid like the rest of them, to the point that in the midst of the storm He was soundly asleep?

♣ Was it because He had enough power to stop the storm?

No. Jesus new His purpose in the world and believed that until that purpose was fulfilled, no amount of storm could stop Him.

5. Purpose provides you with the highest level of focus and improves your mental effectiveness.

Purposes provide you the highest level of focus and improve your mental effectiveness.

It switches you on, takes you and gives you a never-ending pursuit. Focus acts like a driving force that directs your purpose. When you live by purpose, you work in your strength rather than in your weakness. It improves your mental effectiveness because you tend to think clearly without distraction. This is one of the greatest gifts of living by purpose: the ability to set priorities and follow them.

I read a story of a teacher who made a difference by helping his students to identify and live by purpose. One day he opened his mailbox to read a message sent by one of his students and it read, "**Thank you sir, I am now thinking**." You can imagine the joy of such a teacher for improving the mental effectiveness of his student. When you have purpose, your focus is today and not so much about the past because purpose worries about what you can do today to make tomorrow successful. Apostle Paul once said, **"One thing I do: forgetting the past and focussing on the future."**

6. **Purpose will make you unique and set you apart from the majority**. We are all created special. However, you may feel that you have not identified the very gift God has given you. Lynn Johnston, in his book *"Lynn on Ideas"* (1947) said, **"We are all born with wonderful gifts. We use these gifts to express ourselves, to amuse, to strengthen and to communicate. We begin, as children, to explore and develop our talents, often unaware that we are unique, that not everyone can do what we are doing."** All we need to do is to act on the unique spirit that is in us. The Bible calls this an **excellent spirit**. Let us capture an example in:

   Daniel 6:3 (KJV).

   "Then this Daniel was preferred above the presidents and princes because an excellent spirit *was* in him and the king thought to set him over the whole realm."

   > Excellence is a constant repetition of a spiritual habit.

   The excellent spirit, that was in Daniel, set him apart from the rest of his peers. Excellence is therefore the constant repetition of spiritual habit. This Daniel was a man who lived by purpose. He was a slave, young man who was captured from Israel, in the time of King Nebuchadnezzar.

He did not consider his situation but pressed on regardless. This is what set him apart.

Daniel 1:8 (KJV)

"But Daniel purposed in his heart that he would not defile himself with the portion of the king's meat or with the wine which he drank: therefore he requested of the prince of the eunuchs that he might not defile himself."

The key, here, is that the resolve to be devoted to principle and committed to a course of action lies in the unfolding of an excellent spirit in us. When we are devoted to our purpose and do not compromise, we reap the benefit of our uniqueness.

7. Purpose yields in you an internal consistency.

Internal consistency is the ability to demonstrate willingness and intention towards your purpose. One of the keys to accomplishing by purpose is to be constant and stay away from contradicting yourself, especially in what you believe in because the road to success is never straight. Life is a spiral growth so it takes internal consistency to stand like a rock when life gets rough. When you are hit hard and your path seems shattered, purpose will give you what you need to still make it to the next level. Have you ever been in a situation where life becomes bleak so you feel you want to give up? In these periods, a man of purpose reaps the benefit of taking baby steps that leads to a bigger picture of accomplishment. Internal consistency is also agreeing with your spiritual sensibility of what is right and worthwhile. Internal consistency here also means perseverance.

ALIVE FOR A PURPOSE

As you can see, purpose works for your own advantage. The Bible says in Romans 8:26 that the Holy Spirit intercedes for a man who lives by purpose. I am not encouraging you just to try it, rather train yourself to find who you are and what you have been created for and then live from your inside out. God bless you!

KEY LESSONS AND PRINCIPLES

➢ No matter our work or role in life, we should also view it as God's special calling to serve our purpose.

➢ Ultimate joy goes beyond riches. It is living a Christ-centred, purposeful life.

➢ Be conscious of your purpose even in undesirable periods of life. God's purpose for your life will transform your life as long as you stay committed.

➢ Purpose will create in you a recipe for effective living.

➢ The focus of purpose is not the past but today and how to make tomorrow successful.

➢ The resolve to be devoted to principle and committed to a course of action lies in the unfolding of an excellent spirit in us.

CHAPTER 8
THE NEXT LEVEL

One of the problems we face in life is not because we do not have purpose but is because we are failing to take what we have to the next level. It is a principle factor that whenever purpose is unknown abuse is inevitable. This we know but what we seem to forget is, whenever nothing much is done to a known purpose, abuse also becomes inevitable. What, therefore, are the next level and relationship to purpose? At this stage of the book, the focus is towards those who have discovered themselves and are willing to do more with what they have.

1) The next level is the desire to maximise potential. Potential is to possess the power of becoming. Your potential is not what you have already accomplished but rather what you have not. Your next level is therefore fulfilling your potential.

2) The next level is also the **eagerness to add value to your purpose or calling in life**. God's ultimate expectation of man and in fact to everything He created is: to increase. In the parable of the talent (Matthew 25:14-30), *"a man is about to travel so he called together his servants and presented them with one, four and five talent, according to their abilities and then he travelled. The one, with the five talents, went and added value to it gaining an*

extra five. The one with four added value to his and went to the next level, making a total of eight. The man with one, however, hid his for fear of his master and added no value. It so happened that when the master returned, he called back the servants to give account of what each of them did with the gift he gave them. He congratulated those who added value to what he gave them but to the one who buried his talent and failed to take it to the next level, he stripped him of the one he had and called him wicked and lazy."

Please notice that in the Kingdom of God He can take from the one with little and give to the one with much, meaning that God appreciates hard work and rewards accordingly.

3)   The next level, most importantly, is **your ability to multiply, replenishes, subdue and become fruitful in the things God has given you.** One of the themes that keep running through the pages of this book is this, because it is the first command God gave man, according to Genesis 1:28, so it is very important that you get it right.

God has given you something and He is looking for people who will become fruitful in their thoughts, lips and even in their spirit. We are born to multiply, what even seem, little gifts and passions and even replenish your own kinds by reaching out to others and bringing out what is also in them. Do you know that when you go to the next level and excel, you help others to discover themselves? This is what God means to replenish and subdue.

4)   It is simply not enough to have a talent, passion or ideas. You must be **willing to process what you have from its raw state to its secondary.**

In Proverbs 12:27 (KJV), the Bible says, **"A slothful man roasteth not what he took from hunting."** The question that comes to mind is this:

❖   **How can God call a hunter, who goes to farm and kill a game, lazy?**

❖   **What about the one who does not go at all?**

❖   **Does this mean that both the man who fails to discover himself and the one who discovers but fails to take his purpose to the next level are all considered lazy or wicked before God?**

I am afraid the answer is, YES. This explains why, when Esau the hunter, according to Genesis 25:29, had returned home from the forest, with a game, but failed

> God expects nothing from his people than pure fruitfulness and productivity in our talents, gifts and what we have hunted down.

to roast what he took from hunting, his younger brother was able to deceive him. 'Roast', here, is a process of turning something from its raw state to a more advanced secondary level. For instance, imagine yourself buying your favourite meet from the market in its raw state. The reality is, you cannot serve dinner to your family with this raw meat. You first have to process it in your grill or deep fryer after you have spiced it to taste. The grilled or fried meat is what you then serve to your family and not the meat in its raw state. This is the roasting process.

ALIVE FOR A PURPOSE

In the same way, God expects you to add value to what He has given you, in its raw state. Why, you may ask? This is because **"we can't become what we need by remaining what we are. In the sea of mediocrity, just knowing what to do and making effort to pursue it, distinguishes you from almost everybody else."** (Max Depree). I came across a phrase from Nikos Mourko Giannis (2006) which stated that, **"Ideas are like trees, falling silently, in the forest. If they are not put into action, they might disappear. What is potent about purpose is that history is rich with examples of men and women who took their ideas and solidly forged ahead, carving out great success for their enterprises and immortality for themselves."**

Earlier on, in the chapter *On Purpose Person*, we drew lessons from the servant of Abraham whose purpose was to go and search for a wife for Isaac. Now it happened that he was able to identify his purpose in Rebecca and she took him to her parents where he narrated his story. After praying and thanking God for helping him on the right path, he did something most people fail to do. Let us continue with the story from:

Genesis 24:48-59 (KJV):

"And I bowed down my head and worshipped the Lord and blessed the Lord God of my master, Abraham, which had led me in the right way to take my master's brother's daughter unto his son. 'So tell me—will you or won't you show true kindness to my master? When you tell me, then I'll know what my next step should be, whether to move this way or that.'

Then Laban and Bethuel replied, 'The Lord has obviously brought you here, so what can we say? Here is Rebekah; take her and go. Yes, let her be the wife of your master's son, as the Lord has directed."

At this reply, Abraham's servant bowed to the ground and worshiped the Lord. Then he brought out silver and gold jewellery and lovely clothing for Rebekah. He also gave valuable presents to her mother and brother. Then they had supper and the servant and the men with him stayed there overnight. But early the next morning, he said, 'Send me back to my master.'

'But we want Rebekah to stay at least ten days,' her brother and mother said. 'Then she can go.'

But he said, 'Don't hinder my return. The Lord has made my mission successful and I want to report back to my master.

'Well,' they said, 'we'll call Rebekah and ask her what she thinks.' So they called Rebekah. 'Are you willing to go with this man?' they asked her.

And she replied, 'Yes, I will go.'

So they said good-bye to Rebekah and sent her away with Abraham's servant and his men. The woman, who had been Rebekah's childhood nurse, went along with her.

To get to the next level with what you have or what God has given to you, you must learn to:

Firstly, learn to appreciate God for what has first been identified in your life.

"Live a life of worship and thanksgiving always" (verse 48).

ALIVE FOR A PURPOSE

You need to always learn to thank God for who He is, where He stays and what He can do with your life because not every person in their lifetime builds the capacity to really understand the purpose of God for their lives. It takes the grace of God to even discover your calling because most people die with their song still unsung. He is the foundation, so living a life of praise and thanksgiving is a principle thing if you desire to get to the next level.

Ezra 3:11 (NLT) says, **"With praise and thanksgiving, they sang to the Lord. He is good; His love to Israel endures forever. And all the people gave shouts of praise to the Lord because the foundation of the house of the Lord was laid."** Notice that the first thing the servant did was to praise the Lord for his identified purpose before asking further questions.

Secondly, there should be a desire and a hunger to always reach higher.

He was willing to take his purpose to the next level. In his case, his next level was to report to his master. **How many of us know that there is a master we all have to report to one day?** Just as from the beginning Abraham sent his servant so are we sent by God to fulfil a particular calling after which we will return to give account.

Hebrews 9:27 (NLT) says,

"And just as it is destined that each person dies only once and after that comes judgment."

The truth is: without the desire and hunger to finish the purpose race, you will placate with your talent and ideas. In **verse 55,** Laban and the rest of the family wanted Rebecca to stay longer with them. On the other hand, this would have affected the desire and hunger of the servant to move to the next level. **Procrastination is the killer of dreams and purposes today.**

> It is not just enough to identify your Rebekah (purpose) only to settle for your Laban

Today, most people stay where they are for so long because they are either waiting for someone or someone is dragging their feet. The servant's response, however, expatiates to us a principle to get to the next level. **"It is not just enough to identify your Rebecca (purpose) only to settle for your Laban."** Your Laban is usually the familiar, comfort zone or what seems just good enough to you.

Thirdly, not only was he ready take his purpose to the next level, he was fully prepared as well. In **verse 53,** the Bible says, he brought gold jewellery, silver and clothing to Rebekah and gave valuable gifts to the parents and siblings. This demonstrates how prepared he was to take his purpose to the next level and the value he placed on her. Preparation leads to presentation and if you are not prepared enough you will not be able to take what you have identified and curve success for yourself. Without preparation, ideas will remain ideas and talents or gifts will remain gifts.

Proverbs 18:16 (NLT)

"Giving a gift works wonders; it may bring you before important people"

This means that your gifts and talent will bring opportunities to your life but you must remember that if you are not prepared enough, you will either miss out or do nothing to get that opportunity.

Fourthly, he sacrificed something for something.

Dwelling on the same **verse 53**, the gold, silver and clothing also represents sacrifice. Getting to the next level again involves sacrifice, sacrifice that may cost you your time, money and attention, sacrifice to help sharpen your skills to get you to your next level. Always remember that nothing just happens, things are made to happen and like **Dr Mensah Otabil (2002)** said, **"If you do not sacrifice for the future, the future will never be bought by you."** So be always ready to trade something you have for that very thing you do not have but desire to have.

> **Preparation leads to presentation and if you are not prepared enough; you will not be able to take what you have identified and curve success for yourself**

Fifthly: to take his 'Rebekah' to the next level he first had supper and rested at night.

Moreover, the next morning: Here he negotiated in **verse 54. Why did he do this?** Secondly, why did he not go straight on to negotiate rather than wait the night? The principle here is to **almost never negotiate on an empty stomach.** He was hungry and tired after a two-week journey and like any human being, did not think straight. So this servant made sure he had eaten and rested enough to negotiate on a full stomach.

In our case, we negotiate on an empty stomach when we are not fully aware of the situation, like a student

ALIVE FOR A PURPOSE

who enters an exam room without preparation, or make a life changing decision without first praying about it and gaining information about what to pursue in life. In Genesis 25:29-32, when Esau negotiated on an empty stomach, he lost his birthright, which was his key to the next level.

Lastly, your Rebekah (purpose) is always ready to go with you to your next level when you show the readiness to act. Notice how Rebekah was ready to go with the servant when he had negotiated and demonstrated his preparation for the journey **(verse 57)**. It is only when you show willingness and obedience that you will see how purpose inspires to greatness.

Before we move on, there are two things I want you to note from the scriptures, **Matthew 25:14-28** and **Proverbs 12:27**. In both scriptures, God defines people, who fail to go to the next level, as lazy and wicked. This also explains Jesus' attitude to the fig tree that blossomed but failed to produce fruit. He went beyond calling it names to cursing it and the Word says that in few days time, it died.

Most people have purpose but as **Miles Munroe (1992)** said, **"We abort the process thereby affecting the product."** God wants us to be diligent men; people who are ready to value what we have and take it to the next level. In my study of purpose, I have identified five categories of people.

❖ **Those who do not believe in purpose at all**. Such people fail at the end. Not all people discover their purpose in life. Try to talk to them about something good and they will not listen. They are those who are disobedient to God, the giver of life.

❖ **Those who have purpose but do not want to accept that life has meaning**. This category is difficult to explain. They are individuals who probably are not aware of what they have or what they can do with what they have. They are people who finds things cheap; for instance you are born with a gift or talent and because of that you devalue that gift. Such people can be helped only if they are ready to value what they have been given or they will become like those in group one at the end of their life.

❖ **Those who have purpose, aware of their purpose but do not care**: These are people abusing their purpose even though they are aware of what to do. This is the most serious of all the categories. When you deliberately throw a blind eye to what you know God wants you to do, it becomes a sin **(James 4:17).** This person knows what he wants to do but intentionally decides to go the opposite direction. Jonah is a good example. Read Jonah 1.

❖ **Those who have purpose, aware of their purpose, but do not know what to do**. People in this category are willing to do something with what they have. They are ready to go the next level but need help. Most of you are in this category and with a little help you will get to the next level. If you find yourself here, then this chapter is for you. As you continue to search, ask and knock, the door will certainly open for you. All you need to do is to stay strong. Do not give up because you will find.

❖ **Those who have purpose, aware of their purpose, and making effort to get to their next level**. The difference between people in this category and the former is that while the former do not know what to do, people here know what to do and are already making efforts to use what they have. They are a step ahead. This is the best category. They take risks and initiate on their own, even when no help seems available.

I do not know the stage you are in right now but the truth is, the last two are the stages God wants us to be in. Either you are doing something with what you have or you are ready to seek help to get to the next level. It always takes more than just having purpose. Do you have what it takes? Here is what I believe.

1. Direction

It takes a man with direction to take his purpose to the next level. Whenever purpose is known, there must always be direction to follow. Direction is the path along which you choose as a guide in pursuit of your purpose. It is the intended path in pursuit of purpose. John F Kennedy once asserted, **"Efforts and courage are not enough without purpose and direction."** You always need direction in life. If not, you will just merely drift along. Author **Bill Copeland** advises, **"You have removed most of the roadblocks to success when you know the difference between motion and direction."** This explains why God always give direction anytime He reveals your purpose. Let us learn from this example about Jonah.

Jonah 1:1-3 (NLT):

"The Lord gave this message to Jonah, son of Amittai. 'Get up and go to the great city of Nineveh! Announce my judgment against it because I have seen how wicked its people are.' But Jonah got up and went in the opposite direction in order to get away from the Lord."

Notice that the man's purpose was clear together with his direction. His purpose was to go and deliver a judgment message and his direction was travel to the city of Nineveh.

> **When your purpose is at hand but you continue to walk in opposite directions, you simply end up in the belly of a fish**

So we can conclude that his purpose came with clear direction but he went in the opposite direction. When your purpose is at hand but you continue to walk in opposite directions, you simply end up in the belly of a fish. Therefore, whether your purpose is to sing, dance, write, preach or more get started on the right direction.

2. Develop Values

The choices we make in life and the values we place on our purpose is what determine our achievements at the end. Another key to the next level is to learn to value what you have identified in your life. Values are the core beliefs, respect and usefulness you place on your purpose. **In a deeper meaning, it is your ability to recognise what you have and make necessary effort to cherish it and not sell it at any price.** How worthy do you think your purpose is?

There is nothing like 'of little value' when it comes to purpose. You may only have one talent but the value you put on it has the power to multiply it. Remember Jesus parable of the talents. The one with little talent obviously placed minimal value on it. It's no wonder he could not take it to the next level; he lost his purpose as well.

ALIVE FOR A PURPOSE

A friend called me one evening and asked me to pray with her because she was contemplating suicide. I quickly rushed to her room as she was living in a flat close to mine. Her reason was that she had been unemployed for some months and it was beginning to get on her nerves. She had all sorts of bills to pay including her child's school fees not knowing what to do the devil had succeeded in capturing her mind with such a filthy thought. I prayed with her and left but early the next morning, I went to her to strike a conversation. This is someone who had the natural gift of plaiting hair. With little effort, she could open her own saloon and would not even need to depend on the economy for work. Her problem was that she undervalued what God had freely given to her. Like the man with one talent, she placed less value on her gift.

I encouraged her and we began by simply making complementary cards, which we distributed, to outsiders. In the first month alone, she made enough to cater for her needs and today she is so fully booked that she hardly depends on the government for jobs. I agree with **Nigel MacLennan (1999)** when he asserted, "**When purpose and values does not match there is always a problem**". Esau created a problem for himself when he undervalued his birthright for a mere plate of food. He lost it at the time when he needed it. The lesson we learn from Esau is: "**When we do not value what we have, we sell it cheap**" **(Mensa Otabil 1999)**.

When you identify your purpose and develop worthy values, not to compromise under any circumstances, your destiny becomes exciting. This is because a strong value and an awesome purpose give you more power than those who lack it. That is why some people are able to take their purpose to the next level and others are not. The servant of Abraham demonstrated these qualities when he brought out valuable gifts to the parents of Rebekah. It was a sign of his preparation and seriousness to cherish what he had identified. God is looking to increase those who demonstrate the capacity to nurture what they have into a more valuable product.

3. Take initiative

Begin something, no matter how small it may look. God does not despise small beginnings. Before Him there is nothing like small talent or gift or an idea. Writers write, singers sings, producers produce and leaders lead. You do not get to the next level with what you have until you desire something. Yes, it is a fact that the beginning of a thing is always difficult but it is not until you have challenged yourself and are willing to seize half chances that you see purpose fulfilled. Identify the specific problems preventing you to act on your purpose and deal with them. Whether it is fear, frustration or defeat, be encouraged. The spirit that raised Jesus from death is what lives in you. Motivate yourself and stop waiting for a perfect time, **"for the greatest time wasted is the time getting started" (Dawson Trotman).**

> Failure will never be able to overtake you if your determination to succeed is strong enough

4. Determination and discipline

I have come across thousands of people who have ideas and purpose. The reason why they are not going the next level is not that their ideas are not enough; they lack the power to take their purpose to the next chapter. Both failures and successful people experience a fall along the purpose road. What separates them, at the end, is that successful people are those who rise up from failure and fight ahead until they have accomplished their purpose. **Thomas Edison** was right when he said, **"Many of life's failures are people who did not realise how close they were to success when they gave up."**

> Purpose provides hope for accomplishments but purpose with determination and discipline guarantees your success

Failure will never be able to overtake you if your determination to succeed is strong enough. Determination is persevering, staying committed to a course of action. It is the ability to make things happen no matter the level of an unpleasant situation. Most of the time your ability to accomplish by purpose has nothing to do with your destiny, it has more to do with your perseverance. Picture for a second a pregnant woman in a maternity hall ready to deliver her baby. It takes the commitment to push hard, until her purpose is finally achieved, meaning that if her perseverance level is not high enough she has to increase it until the baby comes.

❖ **How hard are you pushing?**

❖ Do you possess the staying power to work on your calling?

Determination will sustain your purpose. Discipline on the other hand is the secret to determination. It is having the right attitude towards what you want to accomplish in life. Both are characteristics you build over a lifetime. If you are to possess discipline and determination, you must:

❖ **Stop giving up**. For purpose to be accomplished there will be obstacles and that will mean opportunities to go to the next level instead of giving up. **Stop giving up and start stepping up!**

❖ **Be willing to go that extra level all the time; develop that mindset to win.**

❖ **Quit settling for good enough.** It is good to discover your calling in life but it is much more fulfilling to accomplish that purpose. **Don't allow your accomplishment of today deny you your accomplishment of tomorrow.**

❖ **Stop thinking that the road will always be easy**. God never promised the next level easier than the previous level. He however promises never to leave you in the middle of the road when difficulty comes but the road is never easy. Purpose provides hope for accomplishments but purpose, with determination and discipline, guarantees your success.

5. Believe in yourself and the things you can do.

If you must achieve by purpose, you must start believing in yourself. The journey from gaps to significance requires faith. It is one thing, believing in your purpose, and another, believing that you have what it takes to accomplish what you have identified in your life. **Nelson Mandela's** inaugural speech, upon assuming the presidency of South Africa, should have a profound effect on you. He said,

"Our deepest fear is not that we are inadequate. Our deepest fear is that we are powerful beyond measure. It is our light, not our darkness, that most frightens us. We ask ourselves, "Who am I, brilliant, gorgeous, talented, fabulous?" Actually, who are you not? You are a child of God. Your playing small does not help the world. There is nothing enlightening about shrinking so that other people will not feel insecure around you. We were born to make manifest the glory of God that is within us. It's not just in some of us, it's in everyone. And as we let our light shine, we unconsciously give other people permission to shine. As we liberate our fear, our presence automatically liberates others."

Placing a limitation on what you will do will only lead you to limiting what you can do

When God called Abraham out of his father's home, there were a number of specific things He requested from Abraham if he was to be sure of success. One key requirement was faith or belief. An undivided faith in God and a belief in what you can do is one of the keys from gaps to significance, God advised to Abraham. Read **Genesis 15:1-10** for more.

ALIVE FOR A PURPOSE

You are what you believe. Your life will always follow how you think so if you think little you will achieve less or vice versa. Placing a limitation on what you will do will only lead you to limiting what you can do.

After wondering for forty years in the wilderness, a new generation was ready to enter into the promise land but first God appeared to Joshua to prepare him to lead the people. God thought Joshua and the entire nation the key to fulfilling their purpose now that Moses was dead.

Joshua 1:6-9 (NLT):

"Be strong and courageous, for you will lead my people to possess all the land I swore to give their ancestors. Be strong and very courageous. Obey all the laws Moses gave you. Do not turn away from them and you will be successful in everything you do. Study this Book of the Law continually. Meditate on it day and night so you may be sure to obey all that is written in it. Only then will you succeed. I command you—be strong and courageous! Do not be afraid or discouraged. For the Lord your God is with you wherever you go."

Notice how many times God thought Joshua strong and courageous. Four times in this chapter God stressed on the word **strong and courageous**, explaining how important it is to alleviate fear and take on the garment of belief. You too need faith to begin and to continue what God has put ahead of you. To take what you have to where God wants you, you need faith in four areas.

❖ **Faith in God**: Believing in God is the key to discovering who you are. You will have a fantastic advantage in trusting Him. When the task ahead becomes

ALIVE FOR A PURPOSE

tough, His strength will get you through. You possess this faith by reading the Bible and obeying it.

❖ **Faith in yourself**: You need belief in yourself that you can make it and that you are the best person for what is ahead of you. Faith in yourself will practically lift you up and make what God has said concerning you become a reality.

❖ **Faith in others**: Believe in others because people are the most important asset you have. It is good for people to believe in their leader but it is much more rewarding when a leader believes in his people. Without the people you influence, you are nothing. You need others to survive. You can only influence those you respect.

❖ **Faith in your purpose**: No idea is too small. No talent is too little to believe in. Value what you have and what you have will empower you and enlarge you. Live the life you were meant to, for "**if you do not live it, you do not believe it.**" **– Paul Harvey**

KEY LESSONS AND PRINCIPLES

➢ Whenever nothing much is done about a known purpose, abuse is also inevitable.

➢ In the kingdom of God, He can take from the one with few and add it to the one with much.

➢ Both the man who fails to discover himself and the one who discovers but fails to take his purpose to the next level are all considered lazy and wicked before God.

➢ On the purpose route, be mindful of the familiar. Procrastination is the killer of dreams!

➢ Do not just identify your purpose only to stay in your comfort zone. Stretch to success!

➢ Never negotiate on an empty stomach.

➢ The next level of purpose includes preparation, sacrifice, determination, discipline and initiatives, developing values and demonstrating faith.

CHAPTER 9
WISDOM AND PURPOSE

Many people die without unveiling their wealth of wisdom. It is always said that the cemetery is the place with most untouched gifts and talents because many people have died without living their God given purpose. Nevertheless, sadly, we still live in a world where knowledge is plentiful but true wisdom is scarce. Today we either fail to discover or rediscover our purpose in life or fail to act wisely with our calling. Everyday has twenty four hours filled with opportunities: to grow, live and produce something purposeful out of life; yet it is easy to waste time.

Waste has become a way of life for many who live in the land of plenty. We have become bad stewards of the purpose God has

> We still live in a world where knowledge is plentiful but true wisdom is scarce

bestowed on us. You may not be a lazy person when it comes to identifying your calling in life but you may be when it comes to directing and taking wise initiatives to process what you have.

God wants us to make good use of what He has given us and not just to identify them. The surest way to do that is by acting wisely. It takes divine wisdom to build your purpose because when wisdom precedes your purpose you become stronger through good sense. The only thing that precedes your purpose is wisdom and the one thing that will also help you to accomplish your purpose is wisdom. For instance, the book of Genesis explains to us the wisdom of God before and after creation. In **Genesis 1,** we see great and manifold are His works, how through wisdom He established this world. We admire this wisdom, not only through that regular progress of creation but also through its perfect adaptation to the end. This He demonstrated when He said in **Proverbs 8:22-26 (KJV):**

"The Lord possessed me (wisdom) in the beginning of His way, before His works of old. I was set up from everlasting, from the beginning, or ever the earth was. When *there were* no depths, I was brought forth; when *there were* no fountains abounding with water. Before the mountains were settled, before the hills was I brought forth. While, as yet, He had not made the earth, or the fields, or the highest part of the dust of the world."

Therefore, the wisdom of God does not only begin something but also perfects that thing. This same wisdom resides in you because He made you and said the same thing about you.

"So God created people in His own image; God patterned them after Himself; male and female He created them. God blessed them and told them, 'Multiply and fill the earth and subdue it. Be masters over the fish and birds and all the animals'." (Genesis 1:27-28 (NLT))

The image of God is wisdom and since you are patterned after Him, you too should multiply through purpose. You have been predestined to succeed because you have inherited the divine nature of God from the beginning. What this chapter seeks to achieve is that you need wisdom to achieve your purpose because without wisdom, you cannot go to the next level with what you have.

> By whose wisdom are you accomplishing your purpose with, or whose wisdom will you choose to fulfil your purpose?

Ephesians 1:11 (KJV):

"In whom also we have obtained an inheritance, being predestined according to the purpose of Him who worketh all things after the counsel of His own will."

Too often, however, the devil manipulates man with his corrupted wisdom. Just as in the Garden of Eden the devil-deceived man to break God's principle. He is still today using various tactics to corrupt the world. In this information age, you meet people whose actions depict wisdom but you have to be careful not to be carried away. Although they may have wisdom, it might not be the right kind of wisdom. In this chapter, you will find out the two main kinds of wisdom that operate in the world today. The question being addressed in this chapter is: **"By whose wisdom are you accomplishing your purpose with or whose wisdom will you choose to fulfil your purpose?"** Apostle Paul made mention of the two main wisdoms that rule the world, the wisdom of this world and the wisdom of God.

1 Cor. 1:20-21 (NLT):

"So where does this leave the philosophers, the scholars, and the world's brilliant debaters? God has made them all look foolish and has shown their wisdom as useless nonsense. Since God in His wisdom saw to it that the world would never find Him through human wisdom, He has used our foolish preaching to save all who believe."

So we have the kind of wisdom that belongs to this world. Also one called the secret wisdom of God, which was hidden in former times, though He made it for our benefit before the world began.

Wisdom is shown to be right by what results from it

Worldly wisdom defined

Satan controls this wisdom. **Ezekiel 28:12-19** explains the origin and the reason why Satan has become the overseer of human wisdom. He was described from the beginning as the perfection of wisdom and beauty in the Garden of Eden. Even Satan was created by God, ordained and anointed as a mighty angelic guardian who had access to God. It was not until he allowed his great wealth to cause him to sin against God that He was banished from His presence.

"Your heart was filled with pride because of all your beauty. You corrupted your wisdom for the sake of your splendour. So I threw you to the earth and exposed you to the curious gaze of kings." (Ezekiel 28:17 (NLT))

Since then the deceiver has been deceiving man with his corrupted wisdom. His intention is to destroy as many of

Gods original purposes for man. The greatest deception of Satan is to convince man that there is no God. Most philosophers, scholars and the world's brilliant debaters convince the world of this fact because at the top of such is the corrupted wisdom of Satan. God considers such wisdom foolish because it does not fulfil His purpose for man. So, if the results of what you do prove to you that there is no God then such is corrupted wisdom. It is just an attempt to deprive you of God's purpose for your life. When your purpose is motivated by jealousy, selfishness, and abuse, no matter how successful you may have become such wisdom is not the right one. For instance, if you are a young man or woman and your purpose is to lure others to sin sexually, though you may end up succeeding with such wisdom be wary that the devil is the source of what you are doing. You may be gifted to sing but if such great purpose is directed towards promiscuity and creating unnecessary tensions among people rather than praising God and promoting peace and love then be careful because the results of such wisdom are wrong. Satan's wisdom is still wisdom but get it right, it is corrupted wisdom. He perverts your purpose in four ways:

Doubts: The devil manipulates and can cause you to doubt your potential and purpose. He uses fear, frustration and defeat as tools to destroy man; to distract you from God's provision for your life. Do you know that the Hebrew meaning of the word **'worry'** also means **'stress, depression and frustration'**? These are also the number one causes of all sorts of illnesses in the world today.

Discouragement: He (the devil) discourages you from the truth about God with the established wisdom of men that goes contrary to the word of God. He discourages you from your ambitions and consoles you in mediocrity.

Diversion: Satan is always planning ways to distract your attention from the main things in your life. He will do whatever is possible to alter God's original idea for your life. If he tempted Jesus, in **Matthew 4,** then you must watch out. As was with Jesus, he (Satan) attempts to redirect our purpose through physical needs and desires, possessions and power, pride and glories of this world; all to swerve your attention from achieving God's ideal for your life.

Delay: Delaying God's purpose for your life. His plan is to slow you down with sin and spiritually heavy things. Once the enemy cannot get you to sin, he can get you busy on extraneous activities, which at the end will delay you fulfilling your purpose in life. This is why the Bible encourages you to get rid of anything that makes you heavy or slows you down **(Hebrews 12:1).**

Defeat: The purpose of the devil is to defeat you at the end with his corrupted wisdom. The most defeated people are those who lie six feet under the earth with their purpose and potential untouched.

So learn carefully! Satan Is walking in sheep's clothing, using men and women, you meet on a daily basis, just to destroy God's purpose for your life. Yes, wisdom belongs to the aged and understanding to those who have lived for many years but true and divine wisdom and purpose are with God.

Divine/secret wisdom:

God controls this wisdom. This wisdom stretches between you and the divine. **Wingmakers (2009)** discussed *shifting paradigms towards divine wisdom and understanding,* and I quote:

"The divine dances outside of the confines of any hierarchical structures. It is complete within itself and has a singular purpose of demonstrating the collective potential of all life within the universe. It is the archetype of perfection. It is the standard bearer of each soul's innate design and ultimate destiny. The essence of the divine is far beyond mental conception, yet humanity's tendency is to resort to the limiting language of the hierarchical paradigm to define and understand it."

This wisdom is defined biblically as the principle thing **(Proverbs 4:7).** 'Principle' in the sense that it is the **'first and most important'**, meaning you cannot begin, continue or end without it. No wonder the deceiver is working hard to pervert wisdom. God's divine wisdom consists not only of deep knowledge but in the understanding of how to act when matters arise on your journey to significance. It is reflected in the choices that you make, according to His plans and purpose for your life. James talked, in **James 1:5,** about this wisdom. To know God's purposes for your life, to make decisions or take directions, seek for divine wisdom. Solomon is one man who asked for this wisdom. Before he began his purpose, the Lord appeared to him, in a dream, and asked him what he wanted. He replied by asking for divine wisdom and God granted it **(1 Kings 3:5-15).** No wonder he ruled with such wisdom! **Luke 2:52** says that Jesus grew up both in stature and wisdom, at the same time, meaning that for you not to have an unbalanced success, you need both purpose and divine wisdom.

Divine wisdom is also referred to as God's secret/hidden wisdom. Apostle Paul created this awareness of inner wisdom and wholeness when he spoke in the book of Corinthians.

1 Corinthians 2:6-7 (NLT):

"Yet when I am among mature Christians, I do speak with words of wisdom but not the kind of wisdom that belongs to this world and not the kind that appeals to the rulers of this world, who are being brought to nothing. No, the wisdom we speak of is the secret wisdom of God, which was hidden in former times, though He made it for our benefit before the world began."

This secret and hidden wisdom is a gift from God to everyone. It is not for a selected few but for everyone who will access it. The word **hidden** here does not imply that it is **withheld from you** rather it is **withheld for you to find.** I have already explained in the beginning chapters of this book how your purpose in life is hidden for you to find from within. In the same way God's secret wisdom resides in you to find. You may not still understand why but it is God's nature to hide things and your nature to find them. This is what makes God glorious and your ability to find makes you glorious too. God's secret wisdom is revealed to be right because of what results from it. It has been tested and proven since ancient times. By whose wisdom will you accomplish your purpose? I am not implying that you should not trust friends or join a group in your community; this is just to enlighten you of the reality in our world today so that you can make the right choices for your purpose.

Finding wisdom for your purpose

Job said, "People know how to mine silver and refine gold. We know how to put light into darkness and explore the farthest, darkest

If you want to know what to do with your life or have purpose but lack wisdom to achieve it, then ask God who gives freely

regions of the earth as we search for gold. We know how to find bread from the earth and locate treasures that no bird of prey can see."

This is what human wisdom can do; but do people know how to find Gods wisdom?

Job 28:12-17 (NLT):

"But do people know where to find wisdom? Where can they find understanding? No one knows where to find it, for it is not found among the living. 'It is not here,' says the ocean.' 'Nor is it here,' says the sea.

"It cannot be bought for gold or silver. Its value is greater than all the gold of Ophir, greater than precious onyx stone or sapphires. Wisdom is far more valuable than gold and crystal. It cannot be purchased with jewels mounted in fine gold.

Job is widening our understanding to the fact that divine wisdom cannot be found on earth so you should stop looking at man to give you directions for living. No leader can produce enough knowledge or insight to explain the totality of human experience. To understand who you are, what you are doing with your life and why you have been created, our answer must always come from outside and above our mortal bodies.

"God surely knows where it can be found," said **Job.**
Therefore, to have Gods kind of wisdom is important.

I. **Reverence God**

There is a difference between reverence and respect. Reverence goes deeper than respect. Reverence is respect plus fear. You need to fear the Lord. The fear of the lord is the beginning of true wisdom (Proverbs 1:7, 15:33, Eccl 12:13) and forsaking evil is true understanding. Fear Him because of His power, faithfulness, might and mercy. You need to revere God for what He does and can do in your life. He is the author and finisher, creator and destroyer, giver and taker of life and purpose. Your purpose begins and ends in Him.

II. **Ask for it**

You must learn to persist in pursuing wisdom if you are to succeed in your purpose. If you want to know what to do with your life or have purpose but lack wisdom to achieve it, then ask God who gives freely. **"For those who ask receives, those who search finds and those who knock the door will be open to them"** (Matt 7:8). The problem with most of us is that we have purpose but do not persist in wisdom. The verse above explains three different levels to acquiring Gods divine wisdom: **the asking level, the searching level and the knocking level**. For some of us, when we have searched and do not find, we give up or when we ask and do not receive, we lose hope. I am not saying that you always have to go through all the three processes before you activate God's wisdom in your life but when you have tried one and not succeeded, persist through the others and you will receive.

III. Meditation

If you are a child of God, then this point should be important to you. The highest point you can get in your life is to learn to meditate before God every day. **Why do you think Jesus observed quietness before His Father every day of His purposeful life?** He did this to

> You cannot begin, continue or end without God's divine wisdom

receive divine wisdom to accomplish His purpose here on earth. In the same way, if you are to discover, rediscover or take your purposes to the next level, do not just listen, read, or even study the word alone. Learn to memorise and meditate on the Word of God. For in so doing you will receive the wisdom that comes from God. The Holy Spirit speaks when you are quiet to direct your purpose and help you to make informed choices and this is wisdom. It is very important to have an hour of quietness before the Lord every day. It means having a moment of meditation, quietness and deep thought of God's word. This moment will lead you to obey God and through this, you will display wisdom and intelligence among your peers.

> Learn to memorise and meditate on the word of God. For in so doing you will receive the wisdom that comes from God

IV. Observation

Open your eyes and your ears and learn. For when you open your eyes, you ears will understand. Many of us have closed our eyes from divine wisdom so our ears lack understanding. That is why the Bible encourages us to **"go to the ant, thou sluggard; consider her ways, and be wise" (Proverbs 6:6 (KJV))**. Much is said about the need to observe to be an **'on-purpose person'**.

V. ## Walk with the wise

It is a principle, according to **Proverbs 13:20,** that *"whoever walks with the wise will become wise; whoever walks with fools will suffer harm."*

Wise men always say, *"Show me your friend and I will show you your character."* If you have good friends, you will grow wise but if your friends are bad, you will be bad as well.

> The people you choose to walk with or seek counsel from always have influence on your character and integrity

The vitality of divine wisdom to your purpose:

One of the reasons that make this chapter also special is the vitality of wisdom to your purpose. Indeed if there is one thing I will advise you to desire in your life, if you want to go far in your chosen field, is not just wisdom but also the divine wisdom of God. Seek to grow wise in the right direction and it will amaze you how different you will become.

The journey from gaps to significance involves decision-making and risk taking, something that involves more than just having purpose or receiving a calling. This is what makes wisdom a preceding factor in your life. Divine wisdom fills, establishes and acts as a foundation to the promise. There are significant people, in the word of God and in our daily lives, who have acted according to such wisdom; to process their God-given purpose; to demonstrate how vital it is to possess it. They can be helpful models in your own pursuit of your purpose ahead of you.

1.   Wisdom is vital in sharpening your talent, skills and ideas in a completely new level.

Wisdom has the power to lift your ideas into realities because divine wisdom offers an unusual boost to your purpose. It will help you to create something out of nothing. **"Two men were distinguished when God granted, in addition to their talent, wisdom and intelligence. Bezalel and Oholiab increased to a completely new level when wisdom was added to their purpose." (Exodus 31:1-5)**

2.   Wisdom is vital to put your purpose alive in difficult and victorious moments.

The wise learn to take hidden opportunities in the times when the ordinary give up. Because of his unusual wisdom, the young man's (Joseph) purpose stayed alive to shine after his brothers had sold him to die. You may also find yourself in similar situation where there is no turning around. In such cases, seek wisdom and it will push you through. Also, never let either failure or even victory keep you from the source of wisdom. One of the lessons I have learned from the David and Goliath story has been that

ALIVE FOR A PURPOSE

even after such great victory David still pursued wisely. He did not allow that victory to keep him away from achieving God's purposes later in his life. Yes, victories are sweet but stay focussed and forge ahead. In the same way, David demonstrated an unusual wisdom when Saul threatened to kill him. He was able to always stay ahead of every evil plot Saul had planned until his demise. In this case, we can say that David's purpose was kept alive by wise movements and decisions he had made. So in both ways whether in victorious or difficult moments, remember to walk in wisdom.

3.   Wisdom is vital for directing purpose.

"She will guide you down delightful paths; all her ways are satisfying. It is a tree of life to all who embrace her; happy are those who hold her tightly." (Proverbs 3:17-18) The pathway to a fulfilled calling is through wise directions in life because God's divine wisdom will always serve as a guide to your destination, staying ahead of you so that you can avoid pitfalls. The ordinary men, who followed the star to see the newly-born baby, Jesus, later became known as the wise men because they did not just receive special knowledge of what purpose were all about but followed God's direction until they arrived at their destination (Matthew 2:1-12).

4.   Divine wisdom will enable you to use your purpose to bring about greater result and honour.

We are talking about becoming successful in what God has given you.

148   Owusu A Kofi

"When you dig a well, you may fall in. When you demolish an old wall, you could be bitten by a snake. When you work in a quarry, stones might fall and crush you! When you chop wood, there is danger with each stroke of your axe! Such are the risks of life (Eccles. 10:8-9 NLT).

Can we therefore say that because of the risks of life, we stop doing what we are created to do? The answer is, "No." You need to find ways of fulfilling your purpose, even though there are risks attached to everything you plan to do and this is where wisdom becomes the principle thing. The value of wisdom is to make you a success in your chosen field though you may face risk. So do not allow anything from stopping you from becoming the person God created you to be. Bring honour and yield greater results in your life by becoming like a sharpened axe through divine wisdom.

5. Divine wisdom makes your purpose pleasant to watch.

One of my favourite quotes says, "The whole world stands aside for a man who knows where he is going." When a man is wise, his ways are pleasing to watch. He socially adapts and is acceptable by the majority. No wonder when the queen of Sheba visited King Solomon, she was pleased with what she saw. In 2 Chronicles 9:3-4 (NLT), she expressed her thoughts:

"When the queen of Sheba realised how wise Solomon was and when she saw the palace he had built, she was breathless. She was also amazed at the food on his tables, the organisation of his officials and their

splendid clothing, the cup-bearers and their robes and the burnt offerings Solomon made at the temple of the Lord."

6.   Divine   wisdom   makes   your   purpose
peaceful.

From tension to strife, one of our ambitions is to live a quiet life. However, the question is: **"How do we live this quiet life?"** One of the sources is to gain wisdom. Peace is all you need in a world of difficulty today. The peace of God transcends all understanding through Christ Jesus our Lord.

7.   Divine   wisdom   leads   to   a   productive
purpose.

By wisdom, God became productive in laying the foundation of the world and everything in it. Every human being is born with a natural desire to be productive. The only way we can discover, rediscover or take what we have to the next level of productivity is to dwell on the insight of God. Precious one, we serve a God of fruitfulness who expects us to become fruitful too, not only in a particular aspect of our lives but also in every area. Even He instructs our lips to be fruitful with praises and worship.

In conclusion, as you read on purpose, it is important to understand that the one thing that comes before your purpose is divine wisdom and not just any kind of wisdom. If you become wise, you will be the one to benefit. If you scorn divine wisdom, you will be the one to suffer.

KEY LESSONS/PRINCIPLES

➤ When wisdom precedes your purpose, you become stronger through good sense.

➤ Any wisdom that does not fulfil Gods original intention for man should be considered corrupted and of the devil.

➤ The wisdom of God consists not only of deep knowledge but also in understanding of how to act on your journey to significance (purpose).

➤ For you to have an unbalanced success, you need both purpose and divine wisdom.

➤ Wisdom is the gift of God to everyone, especially those who desire to live their calling.

➤ Do not allow the victories of today prevent you from achieving God's purpose that is ahead in your life.

➤ The value of wisdom is to make you a success in your chosen field, though risk is inevitable.

CHAPTER 10
THE CHALLENGE OF PURPOSE
(I DARE YOU TO HOPE)

It does not matter how afflicted your life has been in the past or how shattered your dreams have become. Your skin and flesh may have grown old or even broken with sickness resulting with anguish and distress. You may have been walled in and feel there is no purpose for your life anymore. Sometimes you feel that though you cry and shout heaven is even shut out to your prayers and your path by a high stone wall.

The purpose route sometimes is field with many detours like a lion waiting to pounce on you with its claws, leaving you helpless. People may have jeered at you in the past, scoffing and insulting you because you tried to live a purpose driven life. Life may have been bitter beyond words but I dare you to hope.

I dare you to hope because your ability to live a purpose driven life is not determined by how far things have not worked out well for you, nor is it determined by what people think about you. The source of your purpose is in God and what He has for you is for you. Situations and the

> I dare you to hope because no matter what you have been going through, God is waiting to give you a fresh start to live your calling

works of the evil one can only borrow what God has for you. Moreover, what is borrowed can only be returned back to its rightful owner. I dare you to hope because no matter what you have been going through, God is waiting to give you a fresh start to live your calling. There will be moments in your life when God will stop you on your journey to significance just to breathe fresh strength into you, to help you finish the race ahead.

"It is of the Lord's mercies that we are not consumed because His compassions fail not. They are new every morning; great *is* thy faithfulness. The Lord is my portion, saith my soul; therefore will I hope in him. The Lord is good unto them that wait for Him, to the soul *that* seeketh Him." (Lamentations 3:22-25 (KJV)

The English word **'dare'** simply means **'to have the boldness or courage, to challenge defiantly'.** A friend once told me, 'to dare' is simply to train you to do. Hope is your confident expectation. So be courageous and challenge yourself to finish because God will bring you to an expected end. I dare you to hope because your courage will always be tested. Here is what I mean

1.   I dare you to move forward.

You should not allow current circumstances to keep you from living your purpose but rather God expects you to move forward because what you are seeing now is not the end. I want us to look at the itinerary of the Israelites as they marched from Egypt under the leadership of Moses and Aaron. The story of the Israelites from Egypt to the

ALIVE FOR A PURPOSE
Promised Land is also your story in today's modern world. Their purpose was to inherit the land, filled with milk and honey but before they reached the Promised Land, they had to learn to move forward, no matter the difficulty they came across.

"They set out from the city of Rameses on the morning after the first Passover celebration, in early spring. The people of Israel left defiantly, in full view of all the Egyptians. Meanwhile, the Egyptians were burying all their firstborn sons, whom the Lord had killed the night before. The Lord had defeated the gods of Egypt that night with great acts of judgment!

After leaving Rameses, the Israelites set up camp at Succoth. Then they left Succoth and camped at Etham on the edge of the wilderness. They left Etham and turned back toward Pi-hahiroth, opposite Baal-zephon, and camped near Migdol. They left Pi-hahiroth and crossed the Red Sea into the wilderness beyond. Then they travelled for three days into the Etham wilderness and camped at Marah. They left Marah and camped at Elim, where there are twelve springs of water and seventy palm trees." (Numbers 33:3-10) (NLT)

There are four things I would like you to learn from the Israelites, in relation with challenging yourself to accomplish your God-given purpose.

Wherever you see adversity, you will also see progress. They are partners and when man decides to do something, such obstacles will move

♣ **Firstly, purpose will set you off from one place to**

another.

In addition to what has already established, the gap between where you are and where you ought to be is often not a pleasant one. It takes daring yourself. Therefore, the Israelites set out from the city of Ramses in Egypt and marched on to their promised land. Sometimes, beginning your purpose must be a defiant challenge because not everybody will like to see you live your purpose. Sometimes family members, colleagues and friends will not give you the support you need. Just like the Israelites, the

> **When one remains challenged in the face of adversity, then purpose will always end well**

Egyptians were not in support but they left.

❖ **Secondly, on your on-purpose journey, you will meet your 'Red Sea'**.

'**Red Sea**' in your life represents difficult moments. There will be times where obstacles in life will come your way and sometimes they may seem so huge that you may feel you will never cross but like the Israelites journey have shown us, whenever there is a 'Red Sea' ahead of you, God will give you the courage to cross beyond it. For the Israelites did not allow the Red Sea to restrict them. They crossed it. Author, **John Maxwell**, recalls these moments as "**defining moments of our lives**." They demonstrate to you who you are and who you can become.

❖ **Thirdly, on your purpose journey, it is possible to encounter your 'Marah'**.

'Marah' represents 'bitter' situations. There are moments in life that are not only difficult but also bitter to confront. It can be the death of a family member or close friend which can stop you from pursuing your purpose to attend to such situations. I, personally, encountered a bitter instance in my life when I lost my father, while I was away on a purpose. Such bitter moments happen to everyone in life and the question that first comes to mind is: **"What do you do?"** Defining moments define you. You need to challenge yourself and make a decision because for every 'marah' situation, there is a solution for it. Wherever you see adversity, you will also see progress. They are partners! When man decides to do something, such obstacles will move. In the case of the Israelites, God instructed Moses to cut a leaf off a tree and put it in the water. Immediately, the bitter water became sweet for everyone.

♣ **Lastly, the movement of the Israelites also teaches us that life is not all about-facing difficulties and bitterness. There are good times ahead!**

When the Israelites had challenged their purpose, they did not only encounter the Red Sea and Marah. In **verse 9**, after they had left Marah, they encamped at Elim, where they enjoyed twelve springs of water and seventy-two palm trees. These represent the various forms of blessings God brought their ways as they pressed on to accomplish their purpose. In the same way, if you should remain challenged in the face of adversity, your purpose will end well.

2.   I dare you to challenge yourself!

If you are to make it in your purpose, always look for courage within your spirit and not outside. Most people usually wait for people to challenge them before they come to the realisation of what to do. There is nothing too wrong about waiting on people's encouragement in order to move but what if your pastor, parent or whoever it may be is not there? If you are a person who *always* wait on your pastor, for example, to explain to you the dreams you have, what if he is not available or cannot be reached by phone to explain your dream? You have to learn to dare yourself to move on, most of the time, because something happens when you can challenge yourself in the midst of difficulties. Founder of Success magazine, **Orison Swett Marden**, stated it in this way,

"The moment you resolve to take hold of life with all your might and make the most of yourself at any cost, to sacrifice all your lesser ambitions to your great aim, to cut loose everything that interferes with this aim, to stand alone, firm in your purpose, whatever happens, you set in motion the divine forces the Creator has implanted in you for your own development. Live up to your resolve, work at what the Creator meant you to work for, the perfecting of His plan, and you will be invincible. No power on earth can hold you back from success."

I want to share with you a story of a woman who took hold of her life and stood firm in her purpose to make history in her destiny that has today allowed her name to be remembered in all generations. A man took his wife and two sons, left his home country because of severe famine, and went to live in another country. During their stay in this new country, the man died leaving his wife and two sons.

The young men however got married to women from that new country but, in a period of ten years, both men also died. This left the mother with her two daughter in-laws. After this bitter incidence in the families' life, the mother decided to go back to her home country, since she had nothing to live for.

Therefore, she called her two daughter in-laws, and told them to go back to their parents to start new lives. She blessed them and hoped God would grant them new marriages. She kissed them good-bye and they all broke down and wept but at first the two women hesitated to go back. Therefore, the mother convinced them again and one of the in-laws kissed her goodbye and went back. One however did not look back and this is what she said to her mother in-law, "**Do not ask me to leave you and turn back. I will go wherever you go and live wherever you live. Your people will be my people, and your God will be my God. I will die where you die and will be buried there. My Lord, punish me severely if I allow anything but death to separate us.**"

When the woman had seen her determination, they journeyed back together. When they got back, the woman true to her words

> Sometimes beginning your purpose must be a defiant challenge because not everybody will like to see you live your purpose

began working little by little and after a while, God favoured her to marry one of the richest and humblest men of the town.

ALIVE FOR A PURPOSE

This is the story of Ruth and Naomi. Ruth married Boaz and had a son and they called him Obed. He became the father and the grandfather of David, from whom Jesus, our Lord and Master was also born. Read the full text in the **book of Ruth**.

Now in this intriguing story, we find out how life can be bitter and unfair sometimes but when the worse should happen in your life, does it mean one has to give up?

In this story, I want us to focus on the two married women involved. While one decided to look back and return, the other decided to do the opposite and move forward. There are many people like the one who took the backward decision today. Two things we can learn from them in this story:

1.   **There are usually people who refuse to challenge themselves when it matters the most.**

2.   **There are usually people who always rely on others for encouragement. They fail to challenge themselves.**

Notice how in this story, their source of encouragement i.e. in this case their mother -in -law was not sounding positive. There are times that as an individual, you need to dare yourself to move on in life rather than wait on people whose advice may not be what you need.

If you are to fulfil your calling, then Ruth is the person you have to learn from. Five things you can learn from Ruth:

1.   **She did not allow current problems to dictate her decision.** She was mourning a dead husband, a

heartbroken and confused mother in-law, yet she made a better decision.

2. **She was not influenced by the negative decision of her rival and that of her mother in law.** Right in front of her, her rival had made a decision to go back and her mother-in-law was strongly convincing her to do the same but she challenged herself.

3. **She maintained a clearer vision for the future in the midst of doubts.** She saw ahead and thought of a better life and a fulfilled purpose. She knew that her present situation would not affect the success God was preparing for her. My father once taught me, "**Be a vision able to see far but willing to start small.**"

4. **She took hold of her life by taking risk rather than playing it safe like her rival.** Her decision to move forward rather than playing safe and return home was indeed a difficult one, but such is life. Author **Robert Kiyosaki** said, "**It is risky not to take a risk**". This is true because for her not to have taken this risk meant that her destiny would not have been fulfilled. We now know whom she is in history compared to her other rival.

5. **She remained poised, determined and optimistic with a conviction that was stronger than fear and doubt.** The words of Ruth, above to her mother in-law,

> For you to look into the future to challenge yourself in the midst of doubts, frustration and even defeat, you must remain hopeful

depicts someone who is poised and determined rather than afraid. No wonder Naomi kept quiet and journeyed with her.

To sum up the life of Ruth: She remained hopeful, and hope paid off when she had courage to move forward. Not only did she fulfil her purpose, she also made history in the line of Jesus Christ. For you to look into the future, to challenge yourself in the midst of doubts, frustration and even defeat, you must remain hopeful. Hope is your confident expectation. I have learnt two things about hope. The first is that hope does not give up and the second lesson is that hope does not disappoint. Anytime you become dedicated to purpose and remain hopeful, great things happen.

Lorin Woolfe (2002, P. 27) in his book, *"The Bible on Leadership"* asserted, **"Meg Whitman, founder of eBay, could have been knocked 'off purpose' when her computer system crashed, in 1999. Instead, she worked one hundred-hour weeks for a month until the problem was solved. Fred Smith, of Federal Express, could easily have deterred from the promise land; his blueprint for the company was dismissed as unworkable when it was submitted to his business school professor. But he intuitively felt that using on airport as a hub to achieve twenty-four-hour guaranteed delivery was an Idea that would actually work."** These are modern men who dared themselves to hope and whose dedications to purpose were unwavering and indeed great things have happened through them.

3.   **It is either now or never.**

You must either challenge yourself and your Creator because fulfilling a calling in life is now, while you are alive, or forgotten when you are no more. I admire something about **King David** in the Bible. This was *"a man after God's own heart."* Now the Hebrew meaning of **'heart'** can also mean **'mind'**, meaning David was a man who always sought after what God was thinking so he could think the same. **Can you imagine such a person**? In his entire request to God, he always wanted to know Gods best idea for his life while he was still alive and breathing. No wonder God declared His love for this man even with all his mistakes and failures. He understood the reason to challenge himself and his Maker because to David, God's idea for his life was only relevant as long as he was alive in the land of the living and not when he was six feet under the ground. God granted him his request and until today, David remains one of the characters we all aspire to be. This is how this man argued and challenged his case before the Lord.

Psalm 88:10-12 (NLT):

"Of what use to the dead are your miracles?

Do the dead get up and praise you?

Can those in the grave declare your unfailing love?

In the place of destruction, can they proclaim your faithfulness?

Can the darkness speak of your miracles?

Can anyone in the land of forgetfulness talk about your righteousness?"

Just like David, we too should be challenged and dare our Creator to release His faithfulness and miracles on us while we are alive. Challenge God to help you accomplish His plans for your life because it is now or never. Always be a man of faith and courage.

It is crucial for you to understand that anytime God wants to use your life to achieve a purpose, He can **stop you**. The Bible contains people God stopped before He used their lives. Abraham had to leave his comfort zone. David had to leave his profession and Paul was stopped on his way to Damascus.

Secondly, God's purpose for your life can **stretch you** beyond your limit. Look at the difficult times Abraham had to go through before he became the father of all nations. David, though anointed, had to run away from Saul for a long time before fulfilling his calling. Paul, after the incidence on Damascus, was stretched beyond limit on all his journeys, yet he finished the race.

Again, God's purpose for your life will **send you** to places you may not be prepared to go. **Do you think Abraham was prepared to leave his family to go to an unknown land? What about Joseph? Was he prepared to be sold into a foreign land?** Jonah even, at a point, tried to run away when God sent him on a task **(Jonah 1).** President **Nelson Mandela** had to be sent to prison for twenty seven years before he became the person God purposed him to be. I dare you to hope because God's reason for setting you in

If God did not count you off, do not count yourself up

motion in these directions is for your own good. You may go through these experiences to receive **strength**.

God is always seeking to **sketch** your life to others. I remember when I was a little boy in the primary school, in those times we used to have drawing instructors or teachers who taught us how to draw and be creative. One day our drawing teacher came to class

> After God has dealt with you in life, people will look at their situation and remember yours

and the whole class began to joke and use wisecracks to challenge his drawing abilities. To demonstrate to us that he was the best artist in the school, he decided to sketch randomly one person in our midst out of a class of about forty five students. He took a chalk, stood in front of the blackboard and in a matter of minutes the whole class went quiet, as everybody turned to look at me. I was the random person our drawing teacher had sketched on the board. Seated at one end in the classroom, I could even feel that it was my face on the board. After this incident, no one doubted the abilities of this teacher.

What am I driving at you may be asking? After God has dealt with you in life, people will look at their situation and remember yours.

So you are going through a process in life not only for your interest but also of others. **Hebrews 1:18** says, **"Since He Himself has gone through suffering and temptation, He is able to help us when we are being tempted."**

In other words, Jesus' life is the sketch. We look at our situation today, we see Him and how He pulled through all the difficulties in His life and we can do the same. This is the challenge of purpose and I dare you to hope because through purpose you pose the power of becoming. So as Apostle Paul puts it in **2 Cor. 4:8-10 (NLT):**

"We are pressed on every side by troubles but we are not crushed and broken. We are perplexed but we don't give up and quit. We are hunted down but God never abandons us. We get knocked down, but we get up again and keep going. Through suffering, these bodies of ours constantly share in the death of Jesus so that the life of Jesus may also be seen in our bodies."

So do not look at the process, look at the purpose. Don't look at the things you are going through but the reason you are going through because through the difficulties, God is talking to you about success and through the pain, He is talking to you about joy.

"In between fruit and more fruit are setbacks, in between more fruit and much fruit, there are setbacks but this does not mean you cannot get what God has for you" **(Bishop T.D Jake).**

So if God did not count you off, do not count yourself up. He knows your weakness and mistakes but He is much more interested in your purpose so keep challenging yourself and move forward. The key is always to keep your heart right, rise up every day with a heart to serve God.

Purpose evolves during a lifetime so let us keep discovering our purpose and rediscovering it, in our lives, to experience a sense of joy and significance.

ALIVE FOR A PURPOSE

It is my prayer that the good Lord will grant you the strength to take your purpose to the highest level, as long you are alive. You are created for a purpose. Amen.

KEY LESSONS AND PRINCIPLES

➢ The purpose route is sometimes filled with detours like a lion waiting to pounce on you but always dare yourself to move forward.

➢ There will be times God will stop you on your journey to significance just to breathe fresh strength into you to help you finish the race ahead of you.

➢ Do not allow current situations and circumstances to stop you from fulfilling your calling.

➢ Defining moments in life will define who you are and who you can become.

➢ For you to look into the future to challenge yourself in the midst of doubt, frustration and even defeat, you must remain hopeful.

➢ In between fruit and more fruit are often setbacks and in between setbacks and more setbacks there are still other setbacks but this does not mean you cannot get what God has for you.

CONCLUSION

Precious one, I hope this book has blessed you. There is, no doubt, you are still alive for a reason. As you breathe through this book, knowledge alone is not enough but knowledge with action is what you need now. You need to apply these principles into your life if you want to see results and find a benefit from this book.

Above all, may I introduce you to our Lord, Jesus Christ? He is the source of life and in Him you will find your true reason for living. He alone will help you to discover, rediscover and take your life to higher dimensions. **John 3:16** says, **"For God so loved the world, that He gave his only begotten son, that whosoever believes in him shall not perish but have everlasting life."** To receive Him now, just believe in your heart and proclaim His name with your mouth that Jesus is Lord.

Thank you for reading this book and may you be revived in your spirit, restored in your soul and refreshed in your body. **Amen.**

Notes

Csikszentmliayi M (1990) *"Flow, the Psychology of Optimal Experience,"* New York: Harper & Row.

Jo S (2009) *"Life is Meaningless for young Adult,"* Metro Newspaper, UK. 5th January.

Joni Eareckson Tada *"Joni Eareckson Story."* [online] Available at: http: www.Joniearecksontadastory.com (accessed: December, 2009).

John M (2007) *"Talent is never Enough,"* Nashville Tennessee: Thomas Nelson Inc.

John M (2008) *"Leadership Gold,"* Nashville Tennessee: Thomas Nelson Inc.

Lorin W *"The Bible on Leadership: From Moses to Matthew"* New York: Amacom. 2002.

Mensah O (2002) *"Buy the Future: Learning To Navigate For a Future Better Than Your Present,"* Pneuma Life Publishing.

Myles M. (1992) *"In Pursuit of Purpose,"* Shippensburg: Destiny Image Publishers, Inc.

Myles E (2008) *"Pilots who Flies by her Feet,"* Metro Newspaper, UK, Monday, December 8.

Nigel M (1999) *"Awesome Purpose,"* England: Gower Publishing Limited.

Nikos M.G (2006) *"Purpose: The Starting Point of Great Companies,"* New York: Palgrave Macmillan Companies.

Patrick M. M (1992) *"Walking with Christ in the Details of Life,"* Nashville Tennessee: Thomas Nelson Publishers, Inc.

Richard L (1997) *"The Power of Purpose: Creating meaning in your life,"* USA: Berrett-Koehler Publishers, Inc.

Rene D (1992) *"Mount Analogue: a Novel of Symbolically Authentic Non-Euclidean Adventures in Mountain Climbing,"* Boston Shambhla.

Stephen. R. C (1989, 2004) "The Seven Habits of Highly Effective People," Great Britain: Simon & Schuster UK Ltd.

Wingmakers (2009) "Shifting Paradigm: Divine wisdom and understanding," [online]. Available at: http: www.wanttoknow.info (accessed: 19 August 2009).

Kofi Owusu Amoateng

is a motivational speaker, writer, teacher and minister of the gospel. His vision is to challenge individuals, leaders and corporate organisations to discover purpose and fulfil significance in life. He has a passion for winning souls. He specialises in using sound Christian, practical biblical principles to challenge others to be revived in spirit, restored in soul and refreshed in body.

He currently serves as a minister in a growing church **(RCCG Chapel of Grace, UK)** where he is a leader and servant in three departments including music, Sunday school (Bible studies) and technical areas. He is also the founder of **Purpose Achieving Life**, a group, on Facebook, that inspires people to discover the joy of the new and the fulfilment of excellence.

He holds a Bachelors degree in Psychology and Sociology and is currently studying **Leadership with "EQUIP".** He is happily married to his wife, Rhoda and has a daughter, Christine.